KT-375-092

The Hotel Book

Great Escapes Europe

Shelley-Maree Cassidy   *Edited by* Angelika Taschen

The Hotel Book

Great Escapes Europe

TASCHEN

KÖLN LONDON LOS ANGELES MADRID PARIS TOKYO

028 Amhuinnsuidhe Castle

038 Belle Isle Estate

052 Iskeroon

058 The Lighthouse

072 Charlton House Hotel

080 Spaarr

The Old Railway Station 066

088 Domein Scholtesh

110

Les Sources de Caudalie 190

176 Le Chaufourg en Périgord

162 Bad

Château de Bagnols 166

154

Les Prés d'Eugénie 198

Les Maisons Marines d'Huchet 206

Villa Fiordaliso 258

La Mirande 220

232 La Bastide de M

350 Paço de São Cipriano

246 La Maison Domaine de

344 Palace Hotel da Curia

332 Quinta da Capela

310 Monasterio Rocamador

300 Finca Son Gener

Hotel Portixol 292

322 Casa de Carmona

356 Reid's Palace

328 Hotel San Roque

Contents   Sommaire   Inhalt

On the rocks...
Icehotel, Jukkasjärvi

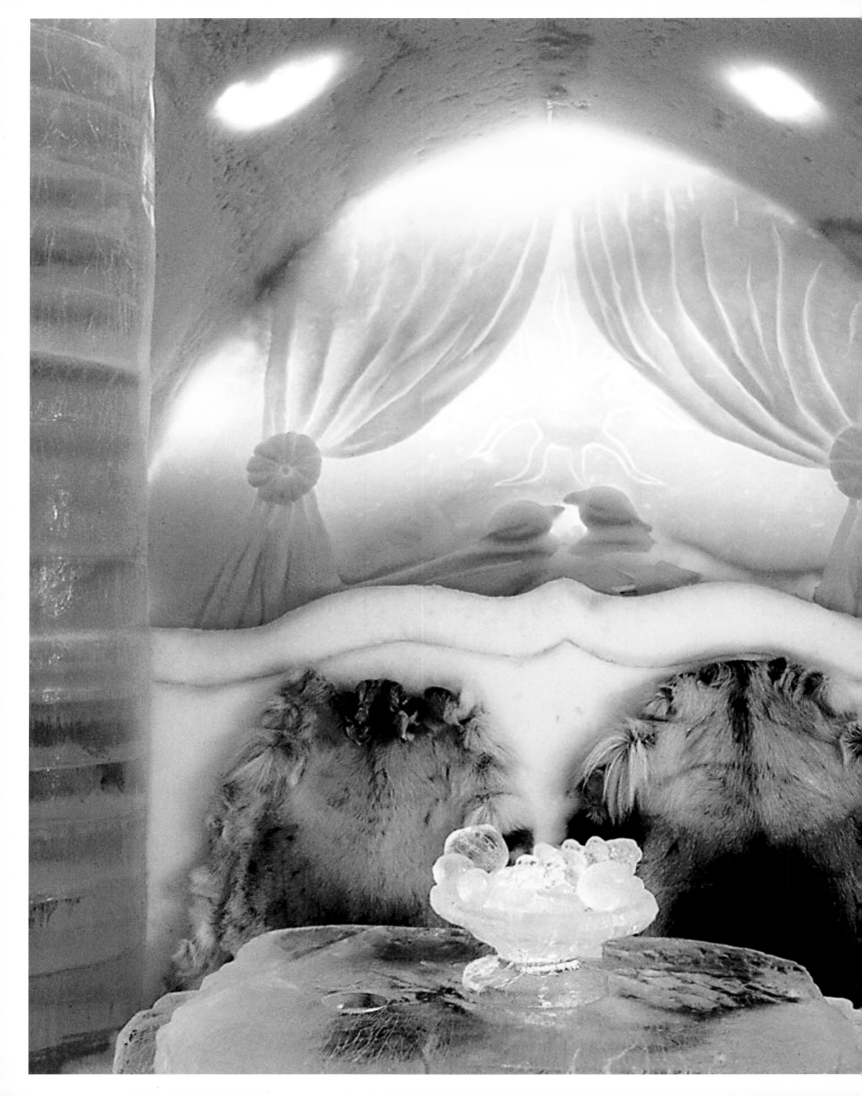

Icehotel, Jukkasjärvi

On the rocks
People flock to this icy place deliberately; experiencing life in an igloo is the magnet.
But this is of course not the usual sort of igloo. It is more of a frozen palace in the far north of Sweden. The Icehotel is proof of the saying that "all that glitters is not gold". Here, all that glitters shows that it is cold, very cold, or else the hotel would melt. And so it does. The arrival of summer sees it starting to thaw and then disappear. A new building is sculpted each year. Ice provides both the building blocks and the furnishings.
Inside, it is 3–5 °C below zero (23–24 °F), which is quite mild when compared to the climate outside. The thick ice is almost soundproof, so that even the noise of your teeth chattering will be muffled. But you'll be snug in an arctic sleeping bag, on your ice bed draped with reindeer skins. A hot drink comes with the wake-up call, and a sauna will bring you back up to room temperature.
Another of its attractions is the opportunity to see the stunning Northern Lights. Starry streaks of colour arch across the night sky in a painterly light show staged by Nature.
Books to pack: "Love in a Cold Climate" by Nancy Mitford "Miss Smilla's Feeling for Snow" by Peter Høeg

Icehotel
SE – 981 91 Jukkasjärvi
Sweden
Tel: + 46 (0) 980 668 00
Fax: + 46 (0) 980 668 90
E-mail: info@icehotel.com
Website: www.icehotel.com

DIRECTIONS	200 km/124 m north of the Arctic Circle; 85-minute flight from Stockholm, 15 minutes from Kiruna
RATES	€ 189 to 299 for a night in the Icehotel; € 55 to 149 in the bungalows; open December to April
ROOMS	60 rooms, including 20 ice suites; in the Icehotel 30 bungalows and 12 rooms
FOOD	The local inn serves delicacies with a Laplandic touch
HISTORY	The Icehotel opened its doors for the first time in 1990 and is built anew every winter
X-FACTOR	The chill factor and Northern Lights

Auf Eis gelegt

Das Leben in einem Iglu scheint eine magische Anziehungskraft zu besitzen, denn die Menschen strömen in Scharen an diesen eisigen Ort. Natürlich handelt es sich hier nicht um einen gewöhnlichen Iglu, vielmehr um einen zu Eis erstarrten Palast im höchsten Norden Schwedens. Das Icehotel ist der beste Beweis für das Sprichwort »Es ist nicht alles Gold, was glänzt«. Denn alles, was hier glänzt, ist eisig kalt, weil das Hotel sonst schmelzen würde. Und tatsächlich beginnt das Hotel, wenn der Sommer naht, zu tauen und verschwindet schließlich ganz. Jahr für Jahr wird es mitsamt der kompletten Einrichtung neu gemeißelt.

Die Temperatur im Inneren des Hotels beträgt -3 bis -5 C°, was verglichen mit der Außentemperatur geradezu mild erscheint. Die mächtigen Eisblöcke sind nahezu schalldicht, sodass nicht einmal das Klappern der Zähne zu hören ist. Doch auf dem mit Rentierfell bezogenen Eisbett, eingemummelt in den Polarschlafsack, ist es schön mollig warm. Mit dem morgendlichen Weckdienst wird ein heißes Getränk serviert, und ein Besuch in der Sauna bringt den Körper wieder auf Zimmertemperatur.

Eine weitere Attraktion ist die einmalige Gelegenheit, die grandiosen Nordlichter zu beobachten: jene in allen Farben erstrahlenden Lichtbögen am nächtlichen Himmel, die wie eine von Künstlern erschaffene Lightshow anmuten.

Buchtipps: »Liebe unter kaltem Himmel« von Nancy Mitford »Fräulein Smillas Gespür für Schnee« von Peter Høeg

Avec glaçon

Un endroit glacial, mais on y va de son plein gré, tant est exaltante l'idée de séjourner dans un igloo.

Bien sûr, il ne s'agit pas de n'importe quel igloo. Parlons plutôt d'un palais gelé, tout au nord de la Suède. L'Icehotel est bien la preuve que « tout ce qui brille n'est pas or ». Ici, tout ce qui brille est froid, glacé même, sinon l'hôtel fondrait. Ce qui se produit régulièrement. L'arrivée de l'été, en effet, le voit s'affaisser puis disparaître. Et chaque année, un nouvel édifice est sculpté dans la glace, murs et mobilier compris.

À l'intérieur, il fait -3 à -5 C, ce qui n'est rien comparé à la température extérieure. Grâce à l'épaisseur de la glace, les chambres sont quasiment insonorisées, et c'est à peine si vous entendrez claquer vos dents tandis que vous vous loverez dans un sac de couchage polaire, sur un lit de glace recouvert de peaux de rennes. Une boisson chaude vous sera servie dès votre réveil, et un sauna vous remettra à température ambiante.

Parmi les autres attractions de l'hôtel figure la contemplation de l'aurore boréale : des arcs colorés illuminent la nuit comme dans un spectacle de lumières mis en scène par la Nature.

Livres à emporter : « L'Amour dans un climat froid » de Nancy Mitford « Smilla et l'amour de la neige » de Peter Høeg

ANREISE	200 km vom nördlichen Polarkreis entfernt, ca. 85 Minuten Flug von Stockholm, von Kiruna 15 Minuten Fahrt	ACCÈS	À 200 km au nord du cercle polaire arctique ; à 85 minutes d'avion de Stockholm, et à 15 minutes de Kiruna
PREIS	189–299 € pro Nacht im Icehotel, 55–149 € im Bungalow; geöffnet von Dezember bis April	PRIX	De 189 à 299 € pour une nuit à l'Icehotel ; de 55 à 149 € pour les bungalows; ouvert de décembre à avril
ZIMMER	60 Zimmer, inklusive 20 Ice-Suiten, im Icehotel 30 Bungalows und 12 Zimmer	CHAMBRES	60 chambres, dont 20 suites; au Icehotel 30 bungalows et 12 chambres
KÜCHE	Das örtliche Gasthaus bietet Delikatessen mit leicht lappländischer Note	RESTAURATION	L'auberge locale sert des spécialités lapones
GESCHICHTE	Das Icehotel wurde 1990 eröffnet und wird jeden Winter neu aufgebaut	HISTOIRE	Inauguré en 1990, l'Icehotel est a nouveau sculpté chaque hiver
X-FAKTOR	Eisige Kälte und fantastische Nordlichter	LES « PLUS »	La glace, bien sûr, et l'aurore boréale

Norwegian wood...
Roisheim Hotel, Lom

Roisheim Hotel, Lom

Norwegian wood

Over the highest mountain pass of all in the "Land of the Midnight Sun"; through terrain that has been etched by great glaciers; with spectacular views of fjords far below, near the town of Lom, is this quaint old farmhouse. It has been here since the 17th century. Travellers who came this way have always stopped to rest here. After a short pause, they would resume their journey. Now, although it appears at first sight to still be an old farmhouse, it is a hotel. Once you pass through the simple façade of this ancient building, you will find there is quite a plush interior. The charming style is one that respects its heritage, yet blends it with modern touches.

Roisheim Hotel is in the heart of one of the most superb parts of Norway. The greater part of this area is a national park. You can see why the wild and beautiful region is called the Home of the Giants. In this impressive landscape are two of the highest peaks in Europe. It seems apt that a museum of mountains is to be found in Lom.

Book to pack: "Dreamers" by Knut Hamsun

Roisheim Hotel
2686 Lom
Norway
Tel: + 47 61 21 20 31
Fax: + 47 61 21 21 51
E-mail: roisheim@dvgl.no
Website: www.roisheim.no

DIRECTIONS	350 km/220 m north-west of Oslo, 15 km/9 m from Lom
RATES	€ 134 to 175
ROOMS	24 rooms in 13 cottages
FOOD	The food is a combination of traditional ingredients and modern cuisine
HISTORY	The oldest building was built about 1550, most of the others date from the 18th century. Roisheim has been receiving guests since 1858
X-FACTOR	Fantastic landscape with breathtaking views

Norwegisches Holz

Jenseits des höchsten Gebirgspasses im »Land der Mitternachtssonne«, eingebettet in eine von gewaltigen Gletschern geprägte Landschaft mit einem atemberaubenden Blick auf die Fjorde, befindet sich nahe der Stadt Lom dieses malerische alte Haus, in dem sich früher eine Poststation befand. Es wurde im 16. Jahrhundert erbaut und bot seit jeher Reisenden, die hier vorbeikamen, die Möglichkeit zu rasten, bevor sie ihren Weg fortsetzten. Zwar wirkt es auch heute noch auf den ersten Blick wie ein altes Bauernhaus, doch verbirgt sich hinter der einfachen Fassade ein äußerst elegantes Hotel. Die geschmackvolle Einrichtung legt Wert auf Tradition, ohne auf einen Hauch von Modernität zu verzichten.

Das Roisheim Hotel liegt in einer der herrlichsten Landschaften Norwegens, deren größter Teil Naturschutzgebiet ist. Sie werden es sicher schnell verstehen, warum man diese wilde, wunderschöne Gegend auch die »Heimat der Riesen« nennt. In dieser eindrucksvollen Landschaft befinden sich zwei der höchsten Berge Europas. Womöglich aus diesem Grund gibt es in Lom ein Bergmuseum.

Buchtipp: »Segen der Erde« von Knut Hamsun

Le bois norvégien

Au-delà du plus haut col montagneux du « Pays du soleil de minuit », près de la ville de Lom, sur une terre sculptée par les glaciers et entourée de vues spectaculaires sur les fjords en contrebas, se dresse une vieille ferme datant du XVIe siècle. Autrefois, les voyageurs sillonnant la région y faisaient de courtes haltes avant de reprendre la route. Aujourd'hui, un hôtel est installé dans la ferme qui a conservé son aspect de jadis. La façade rustique cache un intérieur aussi confortable que douillet. Le charme de l'aménagement réside dans le respect du patrimoine mêlé à quelques touches modernes.

Le Roisheim Hotel se trouve en plein cœur de l'une des plus belles contrées de Norvège, dont la majeure partie est un parc national. Surnommée le « pays des géants », cette région compte deux des plus hauts sommets d'Europe. On ne s'étonnera pas qu'un musée de la montagne ait élu domicile à Lom.

Livre à emporter : « Rêveurs » de Knut Hamsun

ANREISE	350 km nordwestlich von Oslo, 15 km von Lom entfernt
PREIS	Zwischen 134 und 175 €
ZIMMER	24 Zimmer in 13 Häusern
KÜCHE	Eine Kombination aus einheimischen Zutaten und moderner Küche
GESCHICHTE	Das älteste Gebäude stammt von 1550, die meisten anderen wurden im 18. Jahrhundert erbaut. Seit 1858 empfängt Roisheim Gäste
X-FAKTOR	Herrliche Landschaft mit atemberaubenden Aussichten

ACCÈS	350 km au nord-ouest d'Oslo, 15 km de Lom
PRIX	De 134 à 175 €
CHAMBRES	24 chambres dans 13 maisons
RESTAURATION	Une combinaison d'ingrédients traditionnels et de cuisine moderne
HISTOIRE	Le bâtiment le plus vieux a été construit autour de 1550, la plupart des autres datent du XVIIIe siècle. Roisheim reçoit des hôtes depuis 1858
LES « PLUS »	Paysage merveilleux et vue à couper le souffle

A castle of one's own...
Amhuinnsuidhe Castle, Isle of Harris

Amhuinnsuidhe Castle, Isle of Harris

A castle of one's own

A man's home is his castle, so goes the old saying. Would that this could be one's very own fortress, quite distant from the rest of the world.

Amhuinnsuidhe Castle, on the Isle of Harris, is the most westerly castle in all of Great Britain. Built more than one hundred years ago, it stands at the edge of the sea in dramatic and beautiful surroundings. The castle's domain covers many thousands of acres, and is one of Europe's last unspoilt wildernesses. Although it is privately owned, it can be yours for a week. Set in a rugged landscape of mountains and glens, lochs and rivers, and white sand beaches, it is world famous for its salmon and sea trout fishing. And it was here that the weaving of the classic Harris Tweed fabric first began.

This castle on the beach, sheltered at the head of its own bay, is also a citadel of cuisine. Fortunately, for a place so remote, this is a fortress that is full of great food. Amhuinnsuidhe is well known for its cookery school. Rosemary, the television and real life chef, makes full use of the rich local resources – lobsters and scallops fresh from the sea as well as venison and lamb.

Books to pack: "Mary Stuart" by Friedrich Schiller "Ivanhoe" by Sir Walter Scott

Amhuinnsuidhe Castle

Isle of Harris

Hebrides PA85 3AS

Scotland

United Kingdom

Tel: + 44 (0) 1876 500 329

Fax: + 44 (0) 1876 560 428

E-mail: northuistestate@btinternet.com

Website: www.castlecook.com

DIRECTIONS	There is anchorage in front of the castle and a helicopter landing site. Stornaway airport on Isle of Harris, 1 hour by road, is 40 minutes flying time from Inverness, and 1 hour from Glasgow
RATES	On application, for a week's fishing, painting classes, or cookery tuition
ROOMS	8 rooms
FOOD	Judged as the finest in Scotland
HISTORY	Built for the Earl of Dunmore in 1867, now home of the Bulmer family
X-FACTOR	Romantic isolation and picturesque landscape

Ein Schloss für sich allein

»My home is my castle« lautet ein altes englisches Sprichwort. Dieser Traum von dem eigenen Schloss kann Wirklichkeit werden an einem Ort weit entfernt vom Rest der Welt.

Das auf der malerischen Isle of Harris gelegene Amhuinnsuidhe Castle ist die am westlichsten gelegene Burg Großbritanniens. Sie wurde vor mehr als hundert Jahren direkt an der Küste inmitten einer aufregenden Landschaft erbaut. Über mehrere Tausend Hektar erstrecken sich die angrenzenden Ländereien, welche zu den letzten Flecken unberührter Natur in Europa gehören. Obwohl sich die Burg in Privatbesitz befindet, ist es möglich, sie für eine Woche sein Eigen zu nennen. Eingebettet in zerklüftete Berge und Täler, Seen und Flüsse sowie weiße Sandstrände, ist sie weltberühmt für den Fang von Lachs und Meeresforellen. Und hier war es auch, wo man anfing, den klassischen Harris Tweed zu weben.

Diese am Strand, im Schutz ihrer eigenen Bucht gelegene Burg ist zugleich ein Tempel der Kochkunst, der kulinarische Köstlichkeiten bereithält. Amhuinnsuidhe ist bekannt für seine Kochschule. Rosemary, im Fernsehen wie auch im wahren Leben die Küchenchefin, macht großzügigen Gebrauch von dem, was die Natur hier in reichlichem Maße bietet: Hummer und Kammmuscheln frisch aus dem Meer sowie Wild und Lamm.

Buchtipps: »Maria Stuart« von Friedrich Schiller
»Ivanhoe« von Sir Walter Scott

Un château pour soi

« Mon chez-moi est mon château » dit un proverbe britannique. Qui n'a pas rêvé parfois de posséder sa propre forteresse et de vivre dans un château, loin du reste du monde ... Amhuinnsuidhe Castle, sur l'île de Harris, est le château situé le plus à l'ouest de la Grande-Bretagne. Construit il y a plus d'un siècle, il se dresse au bord de la mer, à l'abri d'une baie privative, dans un environnement de toute beauté. Le domaine, qui couvre quelques milliers d'hectares, est l'un des derniers sanctuaires sauvages d'Europe. Bien que privée, cette demeure seigneuriale peut être la vôtre pendant une semaine. Nichée dans un rude paysage de montagnes, de glens, de lochs, de rivières et de plages de sable blanc, elle jouit d'une renommée internationale pour la pêche au saumon et à la truite de mer. C'est également ici que naquirent les célèbres filatures Harris Tweed.

Le château est en outre réputé pour sa gastronomie. Malgré son grand isolement, il offre une table délicieuse et est aussi très connu pour ses cours de cuisine. Rosemary, chef cuisinier à la télévision comme dans la vie, tire pleinement profit des nombreuses ressources locales – les homards, les coquilles Saint-Jacques, l'agneau et le gibier.

Livres à emporter : « Marie Stuart » de Friedrich Schiller
« Ivanhoé » de Sir Walter Scott

ANREISE	Die Burg verfügt über eigene Ankerplätze und einen Hubschrauberlandeplatz. Von Inverness bis Stornaway Airport auf der Isle of Harris 40 Minuten, von Glasgow eine Stunde Flugzeit; vom Stornaway Airport 1 Stunde Fahrt
PREIS	Auf Anfrage, für eine Woche Angeln, Malunterricht oder Kochkurse
ZIMMER	8 Zimmer
KÜCHE	Sie gilt als die beste in ganz Schottland
GESCHICHTE	Im Jahre 1867 für den Earl of Dunmore erbaut, heute im Besitz der Familie Bulmer
X-FAKTOR	Romantische Einsamkeit und malerische Landschaft

ACCÈS	Il existe un mouillage devant le château et un héliport. L'aéroport de Stornaway sur l'île de Harris est à une heure de route ; il relie Inverness en 40 minutes et Glasgow en 1 heure
PRIX	Varient selon la formule pour une semaine de pêche, de cours de peinture ou de cours de cuisine
CHAMBRES	8 chambres
RESTAURATION	Considérée comme la meilleure d'Écosse
HISTOIRE	Construit en 1867 pour le duc de Dunmore, aujourd'hui en possession de la famille Bulmer
LES « PLUS »	Isolement romantique et paysage grandiose

The luck of the Irish...
Belle Isle Estate, Fermanagh

Belle Isle Estate, Fermanagh

The luck of the Irish

Whether you are fond of a cottage or a castle; like simplicity or luxury; casting for fish or seeing the sights, you can choose either, or both, at this place.

This is an alternative view of Northern Ireland, quite unlike the one that is more often shown. There are no "troubles" here; harmony, not friction, is to be found in this quiet corner of the "Emerald Isle". The Belle Isle Estate is set apart from the mainland; a bridge leads to this hidden treasure. Spread over several islands on the lake of Lough Erne, Belle Isle is true to its name. This peaceful place is blessed with scenery to gladden the eye and the heart. Its natural beauty ought to cheer up even the most jaded.

A working farm on waters where the fishing is famed, Belle Isle is one of the most historic sites in Ulster. It has been inhabited since the 11th century, when the first voyagers came to these shores. Bird life, too, has been shrewd enough to throng here. For your sojourn in this serene setting, you can nest in one of the charming cottages; stay in what was once the coach house; or move into the grand old Mansion House.

Book to pack: "Nora" by Brenda Maddox

Belle Isle Estate	
Lisbellaw	
Enniskillen	
Co. Fermanagh BT94 5HF	
Northern Ireland	
Tel: + 44 (0) 28 66387231	
Fax: + 44 (0) 28 66387261	
E-mail: accommodation@belleisle-estate.com	
Website: www.belleisle-estate.com	

DIRECTIONS	115 km/71 m southwest of Belfast, 1.5 hours drive
RATES	Cottages, courtyard apartments, and coach house from £ 85 for a 3-night weekend to £ 460 for a week; from £ 500 a weekend to £ 2000 per week for the Mansion House
ROOMS	4 cottages, 2 apartments in the coach house, 8 courtyard apartments, and 9 rooms in the Hamilton Wing of the Mansion House
FOOD	Self-catering except for those staying in the Mansion House
HISTORY	Opened in 1992
X-FACTOR	Classic landscapes of Ireland at its greenest

Grüne Insel der Glückseligkeit

Egal ob Sie es schlicht oder luxuriös mögen, ob Sie lieber
angeln gehen oder Sehenswürdigkeiten besichtigen – an
diesem Ort können Sie sich für das eine oder das andere
oder auch für beides entscheiden.

Nordirland präsentiert sich hier in einem ganz anderen
Licht, als man es gewöhnt ist. Es gibt keine »Unruhen«,
sondern nichts als Harmonie in diesem stillen Winkel.
Die Belle Isle ist eine Inselgruppe im Lake of Lough Erne,
die hält, was ihr Name verspricht. Vom Festland aus führt
eine Brücke zu diesem gut verborgenen Juwel, dessen friedliche Atmosphäre und landschaftliche Schönheit das Auge
erfreuen und das Herz erquicken. Und mag man noch so
erschöpft sein, beim Anblick dieser überwältigenden Natur
wird einem unwillkürlich leicht ums Herz.
Der Gutshof von Belle Isle, der für den Fischfang berühmt
ist, gehört zu den ältesten Sehenswürdigkeiten von Ulster.
Bereits im 11. Jahrhundert wurden die Inseln besiedelt und
auch Vögel haben sich hier scharenweise einquartiert.
Für Ihren Aufenthalt in diesem herrlichen Naturparadies
können Sie entweder eines der zauberhaften Häuschen
wählen, die einstige Remise oder aber das große alte
Herrenhaus.

Buchtipp: »Nora« von Brenda Maddox

Bonheur irlandais

Que vous soyez amateur de cottage ou de château, que vous
aimiez la simplicité ou le luxe, la pêche ou les excursions
culturelles, vous trouverez l'un et l'autre dans ce merveilleux
endroit.

C'est une facette de l'Irlande du Nord très éloignée de celle
que l'on a l'habitude de voir. Point de « troubles » ni de
violence ici ; une paisible harmonie règne dans ce petit coin
de « l'île d'émeraude ». Le domaine de Belle Isle se trouve
au large de la terre ferme : on rejoint ce trésor caché par un
pont. Couvrant plusieurs îles du lac de Lough Erne, au cœur
d'un environnement enchanteur, Belle Isle mérite bien son
nom tant il est vrai que sa beauté naturelle réjouira les plus
blasés d'entre vous.
Exploitation agricole prospère, au bord d'une eau poisson-
neuse, Belle Isle est l'un des plus anciens sites de l'Ulster.
Il est habité depuis le XIe siècle, époque à laquelle ses rives
furent découvertes. Une multitude d'oiseaux y a également
élu domicile. Pour séjourner dans ce cadre paisible, vous
avez le choix entre de charmants cottages, l'ancienne remise
de voitures à cheval ou l'imposant manoir.

Livre à emporter : « Nora » de Brenda Maddox

ANREISE	115 km bzw. 1,5 Autostunden südwestlich von Belfast
PREIS	Häuschen, Apartments und Remise ab 85 £ für ein verlängertes Wochenende, bis 460 £ für eine Woche; ab 500 £ für ein Wochenende bis 2000 £ für eine Woche im Herrenhaus
ZIMMER	4 Häuschen, 2 Apartments in der Remise, 8 Apartments und 9 Zimmer im Hamilton-Flügel des Herrenhauses
KÜCHE	Selbstverpflegung außer im Herrenhaus
GESCHICHTE	Geöffnet seit 1992
X-FAKTOR	Klassischgrüne Landschaft Irlands

ACCÈS	À 115 km sud-ouest de Belfast, soit 1 heure 30 de route
PRIX	Cottages, studios sur cour et remise de 85 £ pour un week-end à 460 £ la semaine ; de 500 £ le week-end à 2000 £ la semaine dans le manoir
CHAMBRES	4 cottages, 2 studios dans la remise, 8 studios sur cour et 9 chambres dans l'aile Hamilton du manoir
RESTAURATION	Cuisine à faire soi-même excepté au manoir
HISTOIRE	Ouvert en 1992
LES « PLUS »	Paysages classiques de la verte Irlande

Bird's-eye view...
Iskeroon, Kerry

Iskeroon, Kerry

Bird's-eye view

There are few places with a view that can match this one. The beguiling outlook is to be had from Iskeroon, one of the most secluded places to stay in Ireland. The house boasts a spectacular view of Derrynane Bay, and out in the distance, the island of Skelligs. The island was once the site of a medieval monastic settlement. Now it is home to huge colonies of nesting seabirds. For those seeking to settle for a time somewhere more comfortable than a rock ledge, Iskeroon is ideal. Any ruffled feathers will soon to be smoothed down by a few days in this peaceful guesthouse, itself a design jewel in a truly glorious setting. Iskeroon lies in the middle of a lush sub-tropical garden, laid out in the 1930s. It includes many quite remarkable plants, like tree ferns and the very rare Kerry Lily. The path goes down to a private jetty and guests are welcome to go with the owners as they check their shrimp and lobster pots. Nearby is Caherdaniel, a quiet yet colourful village. Most importantly, it has a couple of pubs and a good restaurant. Aside from the scenery – which makes walking an obvious choice – there are opportunities to explore the surrounding hills and beaches on horseback.
Book to pack: "Angela's Ashes: A Memoir of a Childhood" by Frank McCourt

Iskeroon

Caherdaniel

Derrynane

County Kerry

Ireland

Tel: + 353 (0) 66 9475119

Fax: + 353 (0) 66 9475488

E-mail: info@iskeroon.com

Website: www.iskeroon.com

DIRECTIONS	1.5 hours from Cork in the south-west of Ireland, and 4 km/2.4 m from the Ring of Kerry
RATES	From € 45; open May to September
ROOMS	3 rooms, 1 apartment
FOOD	Good Irish breakfast will set you up for the day; restaurant at Caherdaniel
HISTORY	Built in 1936, Iskeroon was transformed 1995/96 and opened 1997
X-FACTOR	Bird's-eye view of the best scenery in southwest Ireland

Aus der Vogelperspektive

Es gibt nur wenige Orte mit einem Ausblick, der alles andere verblassen lässt.

Solch ein Panorama können Sie vom Iskeroon aus bewundern, einem der entlegensten Plätze Irlands. Vom Hotel aus haben Sie einen einmaligen Blick auf die Bucht von Derrynane und die in einiger Entfernung gelegene Insel Skelligs. Einst war die Insel Sitz eines mittelalterlichen Mönchsordens; heute nisten hier große Kolonien von Meeresvögeln. Wer sich aber gerne an einem bequemeren Ort als einem Felsvorsprung ausruhen möchte, für den ist das Iskeroon ideal. Schon nach wenigen Tagen in diesem in eine herrliche Landschaft eingebetteten architektonischen Kleinod hat man den Alltagsstress weit hinter sich gelassen. Iskeroon befindet sich inmitten eines üppigen subtropischen Gartens, der in den 1930er-Jahren angelegt wurde und in dem viele seltene Pflanzen wie Baumfarne und die Kerry-Lilie zu bestaunen sind. Ein schmaler Weg führt hinunter zur privaten Mole, wo die Hotelgäste den Eigentümern beim Prüfen der Hummer- und Garnelenkörbe zuschauen dürfen. Ganz in der Nähe liegt das ruhige, aber farbenprächtige Dorf Caherdaniel, das über einige Pubs und ein gutes Restaurant verfügt. Die Landschaft lädt zu ausgedehnten Wanderungen ein, aber es besteht auch die Möglichkeit, die angrenzenden Hügel und Strände auf dem Rücken eines Pferdes zu erkunden.

Buchtipp: »Die Asche meiner Mutter. Irische Erinnerungen« von Frank McCourt

À perte de vue

Il existe bien peu d'endroits au monde offrant un panorama d'une beauté aussi époustouflante.

Ce panorama, vous le trouverez à l'Iskeroon, l'un des endroits les plus reculés d'Irlande. Depuis l'hôtel, on a une vue spectaculaire sur la baie de Derrynane et, au loin, sur l'île de Skelligs. Abritant jadis un monastère médiéval, l'île est aujourd'hui peuplée d'immenses colonies d'oiseaux marins. Pour ceux qui rêvent de passer un séjour plus agréable que sur la crête d'une corniche rocheuse, l'Iskeroon est l'endroit idéal.

Cette paisible pension de famille est un véritable petit bijou d'architecture, serti dans un sompteux écrin : un luxuriant jardin subtropical dessiné dans les années 1930. On y trouve des plantes remarquables, telles les fougères arborescentes et le rarissime simethis à feuilles plates. Le chemin descend jusqu'à une jetée privée, où les propriétaires possèdent des casiers à crevettes et à homards. Caherdaniel, un joli petit village réputé pour ses pubs et son bon restaurant, se trouve à proximité. Hormis les randonnées à pied, l'équitation est un autre moyen d'explorer les collines et plages environnantes.

Livre à emporter : « Les Cendres d'Angela : une enfance irlandaise » de Frank McCourt

ANREISE	1, 5 Stunden von Cork im Südwesten Irlands und 4 km vom Ring of Kerry entfernt
PREIS	Ab 45 €, von Mai bis September geöffnet
ZIMMER	3 Zimmer, 1 Apartment
KÜCHE	Reichhaltiges irisches Frühstück, Restaurant in Caherdaniel
GESCHICHTE	1936 erbaut, 1995/96 umgebaut und 1997 eröffnet
X-FAKTOR	Atemberaubender Ausblick auf die schönste Landschaft im Südwesten Irlands

ACCÈS	À 1 heure 30 de Cork au sud-ouest de l'Irlande, et à 4 km du Ring of Kerry
PRIX	À partir de 45 € ; ouvert de mai à septembre
CHAMBRES	3 chambres et 1 studio
RESTAURATION	Bon et copieux petit déjeuner irlandais ; restaurant à Caherdaniel
HISTOIRE	Construit en 1936, transformé en 1995/96 et ouvert en 1997
LES « PLUS »	Vue panoramique sur le plus beau paysage du sud-ouest de l'Irlande

A Welsh panorama...
The Lighthouse, Llandudno

The Lighthouse, Llandudno

A Welsh panorama

Since 1862, the Lighthouse has watched over the waves that roll in and crash against the rocky limestone headland it stands on. Now the Lighthouse keeps guests, not sailors, safe from the elements, as an out-of-the-ordinary hotel. With its fortress-like appearance, the Lighthouse does not conform to the usual tower construction of most lighthouses. However, you will see that you are very high above the water when you look out of the dining room's tall windows and straight down at the dizzying drop some 100 metres (360 feet) to the sea below. The three suites all have spectacular views, from the Isle of Man to the north, to Puffin Island in the south. The lighthouse beacon was removed some years ago, and the glass panelled lamp room it once occupied is now a stunning sitting room, with a panoramic sea view through some 200 degrees east to west.

If you grow tired of looking out for ships on the horizon, you can walk in the nearby country park or visit the seaside resort of Llandudno, where Lewis Carroll wrote parts of his fabulous "Alice in Wonderland". Be sure to be back in time to watch the sunset from this most distinctive vantage point.

Books to pack: "To the Lighthouse" by Virginia Woolf
"Alice in Wonderland" by Lewis Carroll

The Lighthouse
Marine Drive
Great Ormes Head
Llandudno
North Wales LL30 2XD
United Kingdom
Tel: + 44 (0) 1492 876819
Fax: + 44 (0) 1492 876668
E-mail: enquiries@lighthouse-llandudno.co.uk
Website: www.lighthouse-llandudno.co.uk

DIRECTIONS	1.5 hours' drive west from Manchester International Airport, 5 km/3 m from Llandudno railway station on the northern coast of Wales
RATES	£ 65 per person, including breakfast
ROOMS	3 rooms
FOOD	Fish restaurants in Llandudno
HISTORY	Built in 1862, the Lighthouse opened for the public in 1988
X-FACTOR	Keeping watch in your own tower

Von hoher Warte

Seit 1862 wacht der Leuchtturm nun schon über die Wellen, die ans Ufer rollen und sich an den Kalksteinklippen der Landzunge brechen, auf der er steht. Heute nimmt der Leuchtturm keine in Seenot geratenen Matrosen mehr auf, sondern beherbergt ein Hotel der ganz besonderen Art. Von außen wirkt The Lighthouse eher wie eine Festung als wie ein gewöhnlicher Leuchtturm. Wenn man aber hoch oben aus den schmalen Fenstern des Speisesaals hinunter in die Tiefe schaut, wird man sich seiner Schwindel erregenden Höhe von 100 Metern bewusst. Von jeder der drei Suiten aus hat man einen schönen Ausblick: nach Norden hin auf die Isle of Man, nach Süden auf Puffin Island. Das Leuchtfeuer auf der Spitze wurde vor einigen Jahren entfernt und das gläserne Laternendeck zu einem Aufenthaltsraum umfunktioniert, der einen Panoramablick von 200 Grad von Ost nach West ermöglicht. Wenn Sie es aber müde werden, Schiffe am Horizont zu beobachten, können Sie im nahe gelegenen Park spazieren gehen und das Seebad Llandudno besuchen, wo Lewis Carroll einen Teil seines wundervollen Romans »Alice im Wunderland« schrieb. Kommen Sie aber unbedingt rechtzeitig zurück, damit Sie nicht den Sonnenuntergang von diesem einzigartigen Aussichtspunkt verpassen.

**Buchtipps: »Die Fahrt zum Leuchtturm« von Virginia Woolf
»Alice im Wunderland« von Lewis Carroll**

Une vue imprenable

Depuis 1862, le Lighthouse surveille les eaux impétueuses qui déferlent sur le promontoire de calcaire sur lequel il se dresse. Aujourd'hui, le phare transformé en un insolite hôtel accueille ses hôtes, bien à l'abri des éléments.

Ayant l'aspect d'une forteresse, le Lighthouse n'est guère conforme à l'idée que l'on se fait habituellement d'un phare. Toutefois, vous serez peut-être pris de vertige en regardant la mer, cent mètres plus bas, par les hautes fenêtres de la salle à manger. Les trois suites bénéficient toutes d'une vue spectaculaire, de l'île de Man au Nord à l'île Puffin au Sud. Le fanal du phare a été retiré il y a quelques années ; la salle vitrée qu'il occupait est devenue un magnifique salon d'où l'on jouit d'une vue panoramique de 200° d'Est en Ouest. Si vous vous lassez de contempler les bateaux qui passent à l'horizon, vous pouvez aller vous promener dans le parc proche ou visiter la petite station balnéaire de Llandudno où Lewis Carroll écrivit une partie de son magnifique roman « Alice au pays des merveilles ». Mais veillez à rentrer à temps pour admirer le coucher du soleil depuis ce point de vue privilégié.

**Livres à emporter : « La Promenade au phare » de Virginia Woolf
« Alice au pays des merveilles » de Lewis Carroll**

ANREISE	1,5 Autostunden westlich von Manchester Airport, 5 km vom Bahnhof in Llandudno an der walisischen Nordküste entfernt
PREIS	65 £ pro Person inklusive Frühstück
ZIMMER	3 Zimmer
KÜCHE	Fischrestaurants in Llandudno
GESCHICHTE	Erbaut 1862, als Hotel 1988 eröffnet
X-FAKTOR	Wache halten im eigenen Turm

ACCÈS	À 1 heure 30 de route à l'ouest de l'aéroport de Manchester, et 5 km de la gare de Llandudno à la côte septentrionale du pays de Galles
PRIX	65 £ par personne, petit déjeuner compris
CHAMBRES	3 chambres
RESTAURATION	Restaurants de poissons à Llandudno
HISTOIRE	Construit en 1862, le Lighthouse est ouvert au public depuis 1988
LES « PLUS »	Monter la garde en haut d'un phare

GREAT ORME
LIGHTHOUSE
WARNING /
MERCHANT SHIPPING ACT 1894·
57·58·VICT·CH·60·SEC·666·
ANY PERSON WILFULLY OR NEGLIGENTLY
DAMAGING THESE WALLS IS LIABLE TO
PROSECUTION IN A FINE NOT EXCEEDING
FIFTY POUNDS IN ADDITION TO THE COST
OF MAKING GOOD SUCH DAMAGE
LONDON EC8   BY ORDER
              L N POTTER

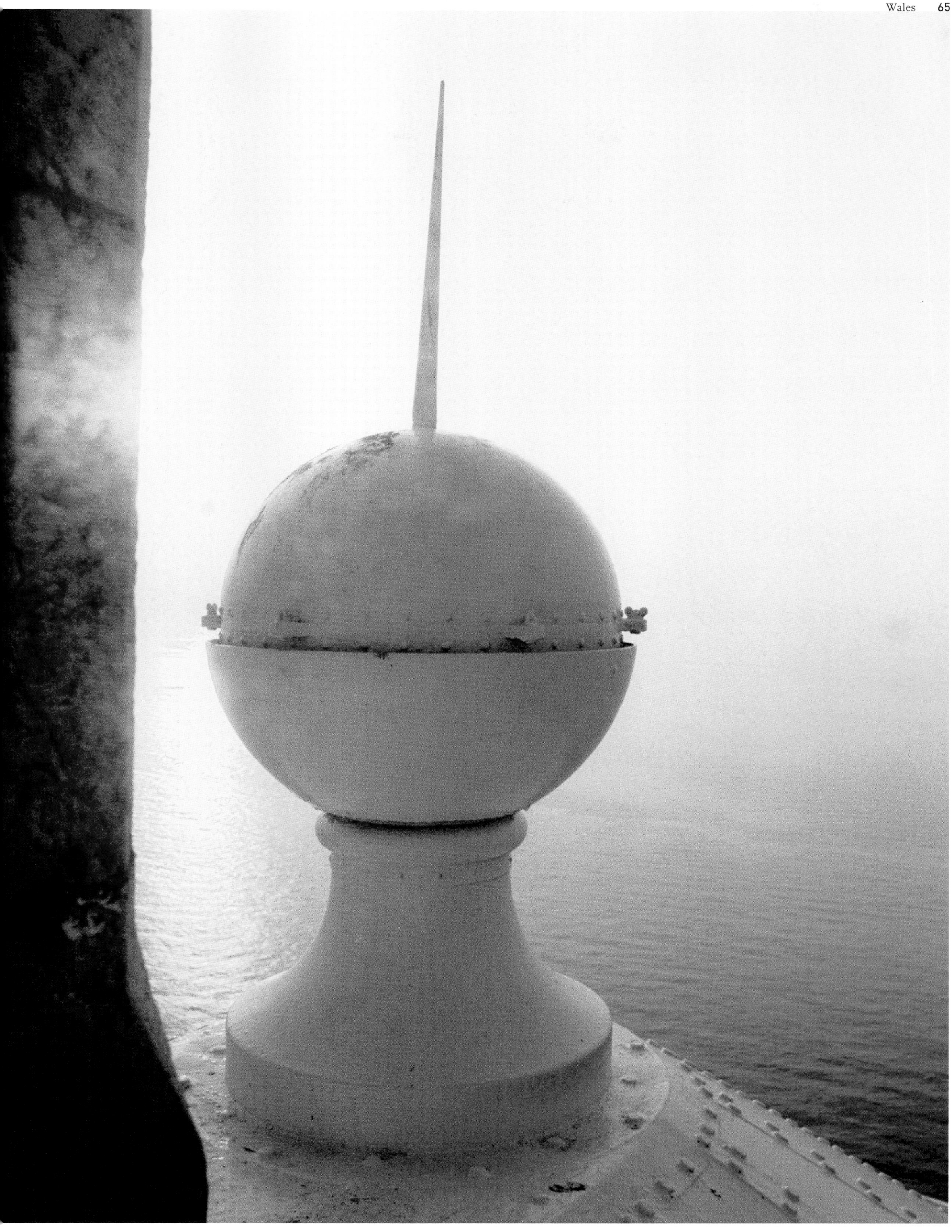

All aboard...
The Old Railway Station, West Sussex

The Old Railway Station, West Sussex

All aboard

Trains never arrive or depart on time, or indeed at any time, at this station. You can stay at The Old Railway Station without worrying about timetables and schedules, cocooned in a motionless carriage overlooking the pretty garden. Trains once went through here on their way to and from London and Brighton. Now the only ones left are Alicante and Mimosa, two pre-First World War Pullman carriages that have been beautifully restored into four spacious and elegant rooms, all with en-suite bathrooms. Bearing no resemblance to their previous life as dining cars, the carriages, with their luxurious beds, plush furnishings, and soft colours, are a clever conversion of old to new. Appropriately, they are located next to the historic Victorian railway station. Guests can choose to stay in the carriages or in either of two bedrooms in an annex to the station, whose former waiting room is now a splendid lounge for guests. There is no waiting on a draughty platform or missed connections here, just old-fashioned peace and quiet. A treasure trove of antiques is in the local village.

Book to pack: "Stamboul Train" by Graham Greene

The Old Railway Station	
Petworth	
West Sussex GU28 0JF	
United Kingdom	
Tel: + 44 (0) 1798 342 346	
Fax: + 44 (0) 1798 342 346	
E-mail: query@old-station.co.uk	
Website: www.old-station.co.uk	

DIRECTIONS	84 km/52 m south of London, 30 minutes drive north of Chichester
RATES	£ 36 to 80 per person, including full English breakfast, served in the station or on the platform
ROOMS	4 rooms on board, 2 in the station
FOOD	A 5-minute walk to award-winning local pub, the *Badgers Inn*, for lunch and dinner
HISTORY	The railway station was built in 1894
X-FACTOR	Living in a grown-up's train set

Alle an Bord?

An diesem alten Bahnhof kommen die Züge weder pünktlich an noch fahren sie pünktlich ab, denn hier fährt überhaupt kein Zug mehr. Sorgen Sie sich also nicht um Fahrpläne und Abfahrtszeiten, sondern genießen Sie unbeschwert Ihren Aufenthalt in The Old Railway Station, in einem der stillgelegten Eisenbahn-Waggons mit Blick auf den bezaubernden Garten. Denn von den Zügen, die hier früher auf dem Weg nach London und Brighton hielten, haben zwei Wurzeln geschlagen: Alicante und Mimosa, zwei Pullman-Wagen aus der Zeit vor dem Ersten Weltkrieg, die liebevoll restauriert wurden und jetzt vier geräumige und elegante Zimmer beherbergen, von denen jedes mit einem Bad ausgestattet ist. Ihre Vergangenheit als Speisewagen sieht man diesen stilvoll eingerichteten Waggons mit ihren luxuriösen Betten und geschmackvoll abgestimmten Farben nicht mehr an. Sinnigerweise wurden sie direkt neben dem historischen viktorianischen Bahnhof platziert, wo die Gäste wahlweise auch in einem der zwei Zimmer im Anbau des Bahnhofs Quartier nehmen können, dessen Wartesaal zu einem romantischen Empfangsraum umgebaut wurde. Vergessen Sie lange Wartezeiten auf zugigen Bahnsteigen und verpasste Anschlusszüge. Hier finden Sie Ruhe und Frieden in nostalgischem Ambiente. Das Örtchen Petworth ist eine Fundgrube für Antiquitätenliebhaber.

Buchtipp: »Orient-Express« von Graham Greene

Fermez les portières

Dans cette ancienne gare, les trains n'arrivent ni ne partent jamais à l'heure : en fait, l'heure n'existe plus. À l'hôtel The Old Railway Station, vous séjournerez confortablement dans un wagon désormais immobile, avec vue sur un ravissant jardin, sans avoir à vous soucier d'horaires ou d'agendas. Les trains reliant Londres à Brighton passaient ici autrefois. Aujourd'hui, il n'en reste plus que deux wagons, Alicante et Mimosa. Ces voitures pullmans d'avant la Première Guerre mondiale, magnifiquement restaurées, abritent désormais quatre chambres spacieuses et élégantes, chacune équipée d'une salle de bains. Judicieusement converties, avec leurs lits luxueux, leur ameublement somptueux et leur décor aux couleurs douces, elles ne gardent aucune trace de leur ancienne fonction de wagon-restaurant. Elles sont stationnées, comme il convient, à côté de la gare datant de l'époque victorienne. On peut loger dans les voitures ou dans les chambres aménagées dans une annexe de la gare dont l'ancienne salle d'attente est aujourd'hui un splendide salon. Ici, tout est calme et repos. Personne n'attend de train dans les courants d'air d'un quai ou ne court pour éviter de manquer sa correspondance. Au village, des trésors attendent les amateurs d'antiquités.

Livre à emporter : « Orient-express » de Graham Greene

ANREISE	84 km südlich von London, 30 Autominuten nördlich von Chichester
PREIS	36 bis 80 £ pro Person, einschließlich English Breakfast, das im Bahnhof oder auf dem Bahnsteig serviert wird
ZIMMER	4 Zimmer »an Bord«, 2 im Bahnhof
KÜCHE	In 5 Gehminuten erreichen Sie den preisgekrönten Pub The Badgers Inn (Mittag- und Abendessen)
GESCHICHTE	1894 wurde der Bahnhof erbaut
X-FAKTOR	Eisenbahn-Spielen für Erwachsene

ACCÈS	À 83 km au sud de Londres, à 30 minutes de route au nord de Chichester
PRIX	De 36 à 80 £ par personne, petit déjeuner anglais complet compris, servi dans la gare ou sur le quai
CHAMBRES	4 chambres dans les voitures, 2 dans la gare
RESTAURATION	À 5 minutes à pied d'un pub primé, le Badgers Inn (repas de midi et du soir)
HISTOIRE	La gare existe depuis 1894
LES « PLUS »	Séjour dans un train nostalgique

Temptations of the countrysi

Charlton House Hotel, Somerset

Charlton House Hotel, Somerset

Temptations of the countryside

"Anybody can be good in the country. There are no temptations there." That was Oscar Wilde's view. But he had not been to Charlton House, which is full of temptation. He would have found it quite irresistible.

Set in the calm of the countryside, this sumptuous hotel has what can best be explained as a quintessential English style. This is because all the furnishings are sourced from the Mulberry Collection; a leading brand of leather goods, men and women's clothing, and textiles for the home. And there is the added lure of a Michelin-starred restaurant. Those with traditional tastes or exotic appetites, and those who have both, can all be well indulged here. As well as the pleasing atmosphere, there are plenty more enticements. At least, you will not have to be persuaded to just relax in the splendid surroundings. Charlton House would be a perfect place to spend Christmas. Retreating here seems a good way to steer clear of all the stresses of the festive season. Maybe you could put this forward as being a most acceptable gift, for yourself. If this is a tempting idea, do act upon it. "The only way to get rid of a temptation is to yield to it".

Books to pack: "David Copperfield" by Charles Dickens
"The Picture of Dorian Gray" by Oscar Wilde

Charlton House Hotel & Mulberry Restaurant
Charlton Road
Shepton Mallet (Near Bath)
Somerset BA4 4PR
England
Tel: + 44 (0) 1749 342008
Fax: + 44 (0) 1749 342362
E-mail: enquiry@charltonhouse.com
Website: www.charltonhouse.com

DIRECTIONS	29 km/18 m south of Bath; 193 km/120 m southwest of London
RATES	Rooms from £ 115 to 225, suites £ 250 to 355; including breakfast
ROOMS	16 rooms
FOOD	Award-winning and starred cuisine
HISTORY	Built in the 17th century, the house opened as a hotel in 1997
X-FACTOR	Ultimate and irresistible English country style

Die Versuchungen des Landlebens

»Auf dem Lande kann jeder gut sein. Da gibt es keine Versuchungen.« Dies war Oscar Wildes Meinung – doch er kannte das verführerische Charlton House nicht. Gewiss hätte er es unwiderstehlich gefunden.

Der Stil des idyllisch gelegenen, luxuriösen Hotels ist durch und durch englisch. Dies ist in erster Linie auf die Einrichtung aus der Mulberry Collection, einer führenden britischen Marke für Lederwaren und Textilien, zurückzuführen. Eine große Verlockung stellt ferner das mehrfach vom Guide Michelin ausgezeichnete Restaurant dar. Egal ob Sie die traditionelle Küche lieben oder exotischen Speisen den Vorzug geben – das Restaurant hält kulinarische Genüsse für jeden bereit. Zu den vielen Reizen des Hauses zählt ebenso die angenehme Atmosphäre wie auch die herrliche Umgebung, die zum Entspannen einlädt. Im Übrigen ist Charlton House der ideale Ort, um Weihnachten zu feiern. Wer sich hierhin zurückzieht, geht dem alljährlichen Feiertagsstress auf äußerst elegante Weise aus dem Weg. Falls Ihnen dieser Gedanke verlockend erscheint, sollten Sie ihn unbedingt in die Tat umsetzen, denn »der einzige Weg, eine Versuchung loszuwerden, ist ihr nachzugeben«.

Buchtipps: »David Copperfield« von Charles Dickens »Das Bildnis des Dorian Gray« von Oscar Wilde

Les tentations de la campagne

« Tout le monde peut être bon à la campagne. On n'y trouve aucune tentation. » Oscar Wilde n'a certainement jamais visité Charlton House où abondent les tentations. Il n'aurait certainement pas pu y résister.

Dans le silence de la campagne, ce splendide hôtel est la quintessence du plus pur style anglais. En effet, tous les éléments de l'aménagement intérieur proviennent de la Collection Mulberry, une marque renommée d'articles en cuir, de vêtements pour hommes et dames et de textiles pour la maison. L'hôtel possède d'autre part un restaurant doté d'une étoile au Michelin, proposant aussi bien une cuisine traditionnelle que des plats exotiques. Outre une agréable atmosphère, on y trouve de nombreux agréments, ne serait-ce que la contemplation du magnifique paysage environnant. Charlton House est une retraite rêvée pour passer Noël, loin du stress de la période des fêtes. Pourquoi ne pas vous l'offrir en cadeau ? Si l'idée vous tente, n'hésitez pas un instant : « le meilleur moyen de se débarrasser d'une tentation, c'est d'y succomber. »

Livres à emporter : « David Copperfield » de Charles Dickens « Le Portrait de Dorian Gray » d'Oscar Wilde

ANREISE	29 km südlich von Bath, 193 km südwestlich von London
PREIS	Zimmer zwischen 115 und 225 £, Suiten zwischen 250 und 355 £; Frühstück inklusive
ZIMMER	16 Zimmer
KÜCHE	Preisgekrönte und vom Guide Michelin ausgezeichnete Küche
GESCHICHTE	Das Gebäude wurde im 17. Jahrhundert erbaut und 1997 als Hotel eröffnet
X-FAKTOR	Klassisch englischer Landhausstil

ACCÈS	29 km au sud de Bath, 193 km au sud-ouest de Londres
PRIX	De 115 à 225 £ pour les chambres, de 250 à 355 £ pour les suites, petit déjeuner compris
CHAMBRES	16 chambres
RESTAURATION	Restaurant primé et des étoiles au Michelin
HISTOIRE	Construit au XVIIe siècle, l'hôtel a été ouvert en 1997
LES « PLUS »	Résidence à la campagne, dans la plus pure tradition anglaise

Home away from home...
Spaarne 8, Haarlem

Spaarne 8, Haarlem

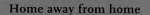

Home away from home

There must be some mistake. This place claims to be a hotel; but it looks more like an apartment that should be for my sole use. But, sadly, it is to be shared.

Hotel Spaarne 8, a historic townhouse, is hidden in the centre of Haarlem. Just a few minutes from Amsterdam, it is well worth the short trip. This is a sumptuous retreat with room for only two couples. Or just a duo, that likes to have the whole place to themselves. One guest, who really wants to be alone, could stay here in blissful seclusion.

Once you are inside this chic environment, one that is more a home than a hotel, there is really no need to go out. No reason that is other than to dine; or to explore the cobbled streets, closed to traffic and lined with sidewalk cafés and many small intriguing stores. In mild weather, there is a private terrace in a walled garden, with a sleek reflective pool to sit by and think. There are delectable provisions at hand should there be need for nourishment; and you can settle in to enjoy the luxury you know you deserve. When it is time to leave and go home you may wish instead that you could just stay here.

Books to pack: "A Weekend With Rembrandt" by Pascal Bonafoux "The Discovery of Heaven" by Harry Mulisch

Spaarne 8

Spaarne 8
2011 CH Haarlem
The Netherlands
Tel: + 31 (0) 23 55 11 544
Fax: + 31 (0) 23 53 42 602
E-mail: info@spaarne8.com
Website: www.spaarne8.com

DIRECTIONS	I don't really want to tell you...
RATES	€ 290 to 640, inclusive of an artistic breakfast and many indulgences
ROOMS	2 rooms
FOOD	Splendid breakfasts at home, and recommended restaurants nearby
HISTORY	Spaarne 8 opened as a hotel in 1999
X-FACTOR	"Aesthetic asylum", in a stunningly restored building from 1765

Fern der Heimat und doch zu Hause

Hier muss ein Fehler vorliegen: Es heißt, dies sei ein Hotel,
doch eigentlich scheint es eher wie ein Apartment, das
einem ganz allein gehört. Aber leider muss man es teilen.
Das Hotel Spaarne 8 ist ein Stadthaus mit langer Geschichte.
Es liegt versteckt im Zentrum von Haarlem, nur ein paar
Minuten von Amsterdam entfernt. Und die Fahrt lohnt sich
auf jeden Fall. Dieser luxuriöse Schlupfwinkel bietet Platz
für zwei Pärchen oder auch nur ein Duo, das mit niemandem
teilen mag. Auch ein Einzelgast, der wirklich nach Ruhe
sucht, kann hier echte Abgeschiedenheit genießen.
Wenn Sie sich erst mal in diesen angenehmen und eleganten
Räumen befinden, werden Sie merken, dass es eigentlich
keinen Grund gibt, überhaupt noch einen Fuß vor die Tür
zu setzen. Es sei denn, um essen zu gehen oder auf dem
Kopfsteinpflaster der umliegenden Straßen zu schlendern.
Diese sind heute Fußgängerzonen, in denen sich überall
Straßencafés und kleine Läden befinden. Bei milden
Temperaturen können Sie sich auf der Terrasse und in dem
von einer Mauer umschlossenen Garten mit einem schmalen
Pool ausruhen. Und wenn Sie Hunger verspüren, steht
Ihnen ein Vorrat an Köstlichkeiten zur Verfügung. So kann
man es sich ganz wunderbar im wohlverdienten Luxus
gemütlich machen. Wenn Sie dann irgendwann aufbrechen
müssen, werden Sie wünschen, noch länger verweilen zu
können.

**Buchtipps: »Rembrandt. Das Helle im Dunkel« von Pascal
Bonafoux**
»Die Entdeckung des Himmels« von Harry Mulisch

Un autre chez soi

Il doit y avoir erreur : cet établissement se dit un hôtel mais
ressemble bien plus à un appartement privé, que l'on doit
hélas partager.
L'hôtel Spaarne 8, qui occupe une maison historique, se
cache au centre d'Haarlem, à quelques minutes seulement
d'Amsterdam. Le détour en vaut la peine. Cette somptueuse
retraite ne peut accueillir que deux couples, ou deux personnes
qui auraient envie d'avoir l'hôtel pour elles seules. Ou encore
un seul client, désireux de profiter pleinement d'une mer-
veilleuse solitude.
Une fois installé dans cet intérieur raffiné, davantage celui
d'une maison particulière que celui d'un hôtel, vous ne
voudrez plus en partir. Sauf peut-être pour aller dîner ou
explorer les ruelles piétonnières pavées, bordées de cafés à
terrasses et de boutiques pittoresques. Par beau temps, vous
irez méditer sur la terrasse privée du jardin clos, près d'un
bassin aux eaux chatoyantes. Toutes sortes de nourritures
délicieuses sont prévues pour les petites et grandes faims.
Voilà, il ne vous restera plus qu'à savourer un luxe bien
mérité et à la fin de votre séjour, vous désirerez sans doute
ne jamais avoir à quitter cet endroit de rêve.

**Livres à emporter : « Rembrandt : Le Clair, l'obscur » de Pascal
Bonafoux**
«La Découverte du ciel » de Harry Mulisch

ANREISE	Ganz ehrlich, die möchte ich Ihnen nicht verraten
PREIS	290 bis 640 €, ein fantastisches Frühstück und viele Extras inklusive
ZIMMER	2 Zimmer
KÜCHE	Großartiges Frühstück im Hause und Restaurants in Gehweite
GESCHICHTE	1999 als Hotel eröffnet
X-FAKTOR	Ein »ästhetisches Asyl« in einem meisterhaft renovierten Gebäude aus dem Jahr 1765

ACCÈS	Dois-je vraiment vous le dévoiler…?
PRIX	De 290 à 640 €, petit déjeuner et autres délices inclus
CHAMBRES	2 chambres
RESTAURATION	Petits déjeuners inoubliables, et restaurants recom- mandés à proximité
HISTOIRE	L'hôtel a ouvert ses portes en 1999
LES « PLUS »	« Retraite esthétique » dans un bâtiment de 1765, admirablement restauré

Sage advice...
Domein Scholteshof, Vlaanderen

Domein Scholteshof, Vlaanderen

Sage advice

Not far from the urban bustle of Brussels is a gem of a country house, one that would soothe the most stressed of bureaucrats.

All those in need of rest and relaxation, not too far from the city, will find that Domein Scholteshof is just the place to get it. A restored 18th-century farmhouse that has been furnished with art and antiques, it is set in acres of gardens. A few days spent immersed in these quiet surroundings will soon calm the nerves; and the cuisine is sure to appeal to the appetite. The chef is considered to be one of Belgium's best. The elegant rooms round out the great menu here. While the restaurants have been marked on the epicurean map, the hotel is the icing on the cake.

Each of the rooms bears the Latin name of one of the aromatic plants that grow in the herb garden. In keeping with the gastronomic focus that attracts its guests, freshly picked sprigs of herbs are more often than not placed on the pillows at night. The subtle scent lingers in the air. A good night's sleep is quite likely to follow.

Book to pack: "Maigret and the Flemish Shop" by Georges Simenon

Domein Scholteshof	
Kermstraat 130	
3512 Steveoort-Hasselt	
Belgium	
Tel: + 32 (0) 11 250 202	
Fax: + 32 (0) 11 254 328	
E-mail: info@scholteshof.be	
Website: www.scholteshof.be	

DIRECTIONS	An hour's drive east of Brussels
RATES	Rooms from € 100 to 225, apartments € 350
ROOMS	17 rooms and suites, 2 apartments
FOOD	The great attraction
HISTORY	Domein Scholteshof has been built at the beginning of the 18th century. It has been renovated and opened to the public in 1983
X-FACTOR	A gourmet "Garden of Eden" – without the serpent

Die Kräuterhexe empfiehlt

Nicht weit vom großstädtischen Trubel Brüssels entfernt
liegt ein Landhaus, dessen Schönheit die Nerven selbst
gestresstester Euro-Bürokraten beruhigen würde.
Wer nach Ruhe und Entspannung sucht, aber dies nicht zu
weit von einer Stadt entfernt, für den ist Domein Scholteshof
genau der richtige Ort. Das restaurierte Bauernhaus aus dem
18. Jahrhundert ist mit Kunst und Antiquitäten geschmackvoll eingerichtet und liegt in einer weitläufigen Gartenanlage.
Schon nach einigen Tagen Aufenthalt stellt sich ein doppel-
ter Effekt ein: Die Nerven sind beruhigt und der Gaumen ist
wach gekitzelt. Kein Wunder, gilt der Küchenchef doch als
einer der besten Belgiens. So überrascht es nicht, dass Gour-
mets das Hotel ganz gezielt ansteuern. Aber die eleganten
Zimmer stehen dem großartigen Menü in nichts nach.
Jedes Hotelzimmer trägt den lateinischen Namen einer der
Aromapflanzen, die im Kräutergarten angebaut werden.
Passend zum gastronomischen Schwerpunkt findet der Gast
abends oft ein Sträußchen aus frisch gepflückten Kräutern
auf seinem Kissen. Ihr zarter Duft durchzieht die Luft und
bringt tiefen, wohligen Schlaf.
Buchtipp: »Maigret bei den Flamen« von Georges Simenon

Sage conseil

Non loin de l'agitation bruxelloise se cache une délicieuse
maison de campagne, propice à une détente bien méritée.
Vous avez besoin de repos et de calme pas trop loin de la
ville? Le Domein Scholteshof est ce qu'il vous faut. Cette
ferme restaurée du XVIIIe siècle, meublée d'objets d'art et
d'antiquités, est située au cœur d'un parc immense.
Quelques jours passés dans ce paisible environnement suffi-
ront à calmer vos nerfs... et votre appétit. Le chef est l'une
des plus grandes toques de Belgique. Les élégantes salles à
manger complètent la carte alléchante. Mais si le restaurant
figure sur l'atlas gastronomique, l'hôtel est la cerise sur le
gâteau.
Chaque chambre porte le nom scientifique d'une des plantes
aromatiques cultivées dans le jardin de l'hôtel.
Conformément à l'esprit gastronomique qui règne en ces
lieux, des brins de fines herbes fraîches sont placés le soir
sur les oreillers. Leur subtile et apaisante odeur vous mènera
vite dans les bras de Morphée.
Livre à emporter: « Chez les Flamands » de Georges Simenon

ANREISE	Eine Stunde Autofahrt östlich von Brüssel
PREIS	Zimmer von 100 bis 225 €, Apartments 350 €
ZIMMER	17 Zimmer und Suiten, 2 Apartments
KÜCHE	Eine der Hauptattraktionen
GESCHICHTE	Erbaut zu Beginn des 18. Jahrhunderts, als Hotel eröffnet im Jahr 1983
X-FAKTOR	Ein Paradies für Gourmets – ohne Schlange

ACCÈS	À une heure de route à l'est de Bruxelles
PRIX	Les chambres de 100 à 225 €, les appartements 350 €
CHAMBRES	17 chambres et suites, 2 appartements
RESTAURATION	L'attrait majeur
HISTOIRE	Construit au début du XVIIIe siècle, hôtel depuis 1983
LES « PLUS »	Un « jardin d'Eden » gourmand... sans le serpent!

Remembrance of times pass

Seehotel am Neuklostersee, Mecklenburg

Seehotel am Neuklostersee, Mecklenburg

Remembrance of times passed

This seems like a place that is kept in the memory, of a blissful childhood holiday; a summer spent by a lake. A place there used to be when one was very young and carefree. Long warm days in the sun and fresh air; untroubled by the stresses and strains that come with adulthood.

This is evocative of that age, where "grown-ups" may recall some of the gentle times of their lost youth. The Seehotel is on the shores of Lake Neukloster; in surroundings so peaceful it is almost like being in a dream.

The hotel's simple design is in accord with its country setting. While its style appears to be classic, there is a modern overlay that makes it more chic than rustic.

Being in this tranquil atmosphere, of white and cream, of natural colours and textures, gives a welcome soft focus on the world. In a boat on the lake, drifting through the reeds; cocooned in a wicker bathing chair reading, asleep, or just gazing at the sparkling water; there is no hurry here, no need to do anything taxing. Whether picking wildflowers, fishing from the end of the jetty, or merely daydreaming; staying here can all be part of going back, just for a short time, to a simpler way of life.

Books to pack: "Flights of Love" by Bernhard Schlink "Elective Affinities" by Johann Wolfgang von Goethe

Seehotel am Neuklostersee
Seestrasse 1
23992 Nakenstorf bei Neukloster
Germany
Tel: + 49 (0) 38422 254 45
Fax: + 49 (0) 38422 256 30
E-mail: seehotel@nalbach-architekten.de
Website: www.Seehotel-Neuklostersee.de

DIRECTIONS	15 km/9 m east from Wismar, 2.5 hours' drive from either Berlin or Hamburg
RATES	Rooms from € 64, bungalows from € 110; including breakfast
ROOMS	12 rooms, 1 apartment and 3 bungalows
FOOD	The restaurant offers traditional rural North German cooking
HISTORY	The house was built at the beginning of the 19th century. During the GDR it served as a holiday resort. The hotel was opened in 1993
X-FACTOR	Back to the way things were …

Erinnerung an alte Zeiten

Der Ort wirkt wie ein Bild aus Kindertagen, als man unbeschwerte Sommerferien am See genoss. Dies scheint der Ort zu sein, an dem man weilte, als man noch jung und frei von Sorgen war und lange, warme Tage im Sonnenschein und an der frischen Luft verbrachte ohne jeden Zwang und Druck. Dieser zauberhafte Ort vermag es, Sie in die glückliche Zeit Ihrer Jugend zurückzuversetzen.

Am Ufer des Neuklostersees gelegen, ist das Seehotel eingebettet in eine friedliche Landschaft, wie man sie sonst nur aus Träumen kennt. Die schlichte Bauweise des Hotels steht in Einklang mit der ländlichen Umgebung. Obwohl es auf den ersten Blick recht traditionell erscheint, ist es nach seiner Modernisierung eher schick als rustikal zu nennen. Die beruhigende Atmosphäre von cremefarbenen und weißen Tönen, von Naturfarben und -stoffen macht herrlich gelassen und zufrieden. In einem Boot durch das Schilfrohr treiben, in einem Strandkorb gemütlich lesen, schlafen oder einfach nur auf das vor sich hin plätschernde Wasser blicken – es besteht kein Grund zur Eile, es gibt nichts, was nicht auch warten könnte. Egal ob man Wildblumen pflückt, am Ende der Mole angelt oder einfach nur in den Tag hinein träumt – hier an diesem Ort gelingt es einem, wenigstens für eine kurze Zeit einen kleinen Schritt zurückzutun zu einem einfacheren und sorgloseren Leben.

Buchtipps: »Liebesfluchten« von Bernhard Schlink
»Die Wahlverwandtschaften« von Johann Wolfgang von Goethe

Souvenirs des temps passés

C'est un endroit qui évoque des souvenirs d'enfance, ceux de merveilleuses vacances estivales passées au bord d'un lac. Un de ces endroits que l'on associe à sa jeunesse insouciante, à de longues journées chaudes remplies de soleil et de bon air, exemptes des contraintes et des soucis qu'apporte la vie adulte.

Au Seehotel, les « grands » replongeront avec délices dans les réminiscences de leur jeunesse perdue … Le complexe s'étend sur les rives du lac Neukloster, dans un cadre si paisible que l'on se croirait dans un rêve.

L'architecture simple de l'hôtel est en parfaite symbiose avec son environnement. En apparence de style traditionnel, l'établissement est doté d'un confort moderne qui le rend plus chic que rustique. L'ambiance paisible, faite de blanc et crème, de textures et couleurs naturelles, adoucit les âmes. Un tour en bateau à travers les roseaux du lac, une sieste, une heure de lecture ou de rêverie, installé dans un confortable fauteuil en osier, au bord de l'eau … Ici, les journées se déroulent sans hâte ni précipitation. Que l'on aille cueillir des fleurs sauvages, pêcher au bout de la jetée ou que l'on se relaxe tout simplement, séjourner dans cet endroit fait retrouver un mode de vie plus simple, près de la nature.

Livres à emporter : « Amours en fuite » de Bernhard Schlink
« Les Affinités électives » de Johann Wolfgang von Goethe

ANREISE	15 km von Wismar, 2,5 Autostunden nördlich von Berlin und östlich Hamburg	ACCÈS	À 15 km de Wismar et à 2 heures 30 de route au nord de Berlin et à l'est de Hambourg
PREIS	Zimmer ab 64 €, Bungalows ab 110 €, Frühstück inklusive	PRIX	Chambres de 64 €, bungalows de 110 €, petit déjeuner compris
ZIMMER	12 Zimmer, 1 Apartment und 3 Bungalows	CHAMBRES	12 chambres, 1 studio et 3 bungalows
KÜCHE	Das Restaurant bietet traditionelle norddeutsche Küche an	RESTAURATION	Une cuisine traditionnelle d'Allemagne du Nord
GESCHICHTE	Das Haus wurde Ende des 19. Jahrhunderts gebaut und war zu DDR-Zeiten ein Ferienheim. Als Hotel öffnete es 1993	HISTOIRE	Construit à la fin du XIXᵉ siècle dernier, le bâtiment était un centre de vacances sous la RDA. L'hôtel a ouvert ses portes en 1993
X-FAKTOR	Eine Reise zurück in die Vergangenheit	LES « PLUS »	Comme au bon vieux temps …

Perfect peace and deep quiet

Landhaus Börmoos, Schleswig-Holstein

Landhaus Börmoos, Schleswig-Holstein

Perfect peace and deep quiet

They say that the air here is more sparkling than champagne; that the landscape is balm for the soul. High praise and claims indeed for the land of Schleswig-Holstein. This countryside between the two seas, the Baltic and the North Sea, is one of pleasing contrasts. Gentle hills, roads lined with trees, sleepy villages, fresh air, the sun reflecting on the waves; this is country life at its best.

A trip to this part of the world will quite likely cause one to contemplate moving here. The owners of this lovely old farmhouse thought that too, when they saw it nestled in the landscape. So they did.

In the midst of fields and moorland, near lakes and very close to the coast, it is in an idyllic spot. Both Landhaus Börmoos and the barn have been restored to mint condition. Under the thatched roof and beamed ceilings are charming rooms with huge alcove beds; once they have got used to the lack of noise these may be some of the best nights of sleep that guests experience. A weekend or longer here, with good food and wine, and pleasant strolls along the beach or by the lakes, would be bliss indeed.

And for those who must hit a ball, there is a splendid golf course nearby.

Book to pack: "Effie Briest" by Theodor Fontane

Landhaus Börmoos
Grüfft 9
24972 Steinbergkirche/Habernis
Germany
Tel: + 49 (0) 4632 7621
Fax: + 47 (0) 4632 1429
E-mail: landhaus.boermoos@t-online.de
Website: www.landhaus-boermoos.de

DIRECTIONS	About 180 km north of Hamburg, nearest town is Flensburg, very near the Danish border
RATES	€ 75 to 95 per apartment, € 10 for breakfast
ROOMS	8 apartments, each for 2-5 people, in the house and adjacent barn
FOOD	Farmhouse-style breakfasts in the lovely old hall
HISTORY	The house and the barn were built in 1876 and the Landhaus Börmoos has received guests since 1985
X-FACTOR	The quiet that prevails

Tiefer Frieden und vollkommene Ruhe

Man sagt, die Luft hier sei besser als Champagner und die Landschaft Balsam für die Seele – ein hohes Lob für das Land Schleswig-Holstein. Die Region zwischen Ostsee und Nordsee ist reich an Kontrasten: Geschwungene Hügelland-schaften, lange Alleen, verschlafene Dörfchen, viel frische Luft und die Sonne, die auf den Wellen der Meere glitzert – so lässt es sich auf dem Lande aushalten!

Eine Reise zu diesem Fleckchen Erde wird in jedem den Wunsch hervorrufen, hier zu wohnen. Nicht anders erging es den Besitzern dieses wunderschönen alten Bauernhauses, das sich harmonisch in die Landschaft einfügt, als sie es zum ersten Mal sahen. Und sie setzten ihren Wunsch in die Tat um. Inmitten von Feldern und Moorlandschaften, in der unmittelbaren Nähe von Seen und der Ostseeküste ist hier ein überaus idyllischer Ort entstanden. Das Haus und die ehemalige Scheune sind beide perfekt restauriert. Unter einem Reetdach und von massiven Holzbalken getragenen Decken befinden sich gemütliche Zimmer mit riesigen Alkovenbetten, in denen die Gäste den vielleicht besten Schlaf ihres Lebens genießen – wenn sie sich erst an die Stille gewöhnt haben. Ein Wochenende oder ein längerer Aufenthalt mit gutem Essen und gutem Wein, mit traum-haften Spaziergängen am Strand oder an den Seen ist wahre Glückseligkeit.

Und wem das zu viel der Ruhe ist, der darf sich auf dem nahe gelegenen Golfplatz betätigen.

Buchtipp: »Effie Briest« von Theodor Fontane

Silence et sérénité

On dit qu'ici, l'air est plus pétillant que le champagne et que la nature apaise les âmes. Bref, on ne tarit pas d'éloges sur le Land de Schleswig-Holstein. S'étirant entre deux mers, la Baltique et la mer du Nord, la région offre de plaisants con-trastes. Avec ses paysages vallonnés, ses routes bordées d'arbres, ses villages endormis, son air vif et piquant, son soleil se réfléchissant sur les vagues, elle incarne la douceur de la vie champêtre.

Il y a fort à parier qu'un séjour dans cette partie du monde vous donnera envie d'y rester pour toujours. En tous les cas, c'est l'idée qu'ont eue les propriétaires de Börmoos en découvrant cette ravissante ferme nichée dans la campagne. Ils s'y sont installés.

Börmoos est un endroit tout simplement idyllique, situé au cœur de champs et de landes, non loin de jolis lacs et tout près du littoral. La ferme et la grange ont été entièrement remises à neuf. Le toit de chaume et les plafonds aux poutres apparentes abritent de charmantes chambres dotées d'im-menses lits en alcôve. Une fois accoutumés à l'absence de tout bruit, les hôtes pourront goûter un sommeil comme ils en ont rarement connu. Un week-end ou quelques jours passés dans cette auberge, agrémentés d'une cuisine et de vins de qualité ainsi que d'agréables promenades au bord de la plage ou des lacs, vous laisseront un souvenir impéris-sable.

Pour les inconditionnels, un superbe terrain de golf se trou-ve juste à côté.

Livre à emporter : « Effie Briest » de Theodor Fontane

ANREISE	Etwa 180 km nördlich von Hamburg und nahe der däni-schen Grenze beim Städtchen Habernis gelegen
PREIS	75 bis 95 € pro Apartment, Frühstück 10 €
ZIMMER	8 Apartments für je 2–5 Gäste im Haupthaus und anlie-gender Scheune
KÜCHE	Gemütlich-gehaltvolles Bauernfrühstück in der hübschen alten Frühstücksdiele
GESCHICHTE	Haupthaus und Scheune stammen aus dem Jahr 1876. Das Landhaus Bömoos empfängt seit 1985 Gäste
X-FAKTOR	Ruhe überall

ACCÈS	Environ 180 km au nord de Hambourg, tout près de la frontière danoise ; la ville la plus proche est Habernis
PRIX	De 75 à 95 €, petit déjeuner 10 €
CHAMBRES	8 appartements pour 2 à 5 personnes, dans la ferme ou la grange adjacente
RESTAURATION	Petits déjeuners « fermiers » pris dans le vestibule au beau mobilier rustique
HISTOIRE	La ferme et la grange datent de 1876. L'hôtel a ouvert ses portes en 1985
LES « PLUS »	Calme et paix

A castle on the water...
Parkhotel Wasserburg Anholt, Nordrhein-Westfalen

Parkhotel Wasserburg Anholt, Nordrhein-Westfalen

A castle on the water

Castles are portals to the past. What stories they might tell if the walls could speak! Those walls, towers, and drawbridges have watched knights and kings in times of war and peace; seen both cruel and chivalrous deeds, court intrigue and romance. Germany prides itself on a wealth of castles and you can still sense the magic of times gone by. Among the most impressive of all is the Wasserburg Anholt, part of which is now a grand hotel. It looks as dramatic as one feels a castle should; complete with moat. The inside is just as stunning with a store of treasures that includes a vast art collection. Hundreds of Old Master paintings are on show. Anholt has a history to match its good looks. It has withstood many sieges; the fiercest of which was laid by Napoleon's men. Much of the castle was destroyed by Allied bombardment in the last weeks of World War II. Over a period of many years, it was rebuilt, brick by brick. Now the great library and ornate reception rooms are back to their past splendour. The dungeon, complete with its collection of armour, is just as grim as it was meant to be.

Book to pack: "Secret Knowledge: Rediscovering the Lost Techniques of the Old Masters" by David Hockney

Parkhotel Wasserburg Anholt
Familie Brune
Klever Straße
46419 Isselburg-Anholt
Germany
Tel: + 49 (0) 2874 4590
Fax: +49 (0) 2874 4035
E-mail: Wasserburg-Anholt@T-Online.de
Website: www.burg-hotel-anholt.com

DIRECTIONS	The castle is situated in Isselburg-Anholt, near the Dutch border; about 60 km/37 m northwest of the cities of Oberhausen and Duisburg
RATES	From € 95 to 180, including breakfast
ROOMS	28 rooms; including suites
FOOD	Gourmet restaurant for all but the dungeon dwellers. Victuals in the old stables for more modest tastes
HISTORY	Wasserburg Anholt was built in three periods between the 12th and the 17th century. Rebuilt after World War II, it opened as a hotel in 1968
X-FACTOR	A castle on a grand scale, with an art collection to match

Eine Burg am Wasser

Burgen sind Tore in die Vergangenheit. Wenn ihre Mauern reden könnten, hätten sie die unglaublichsten Geschichten zu erzählen. Denn diese Mauern, Schlosstürme und Zugbrücken waren Zeugen von Kriegs- und Friedenszeiten, haben Rittern und Königen bei grausamen und ritterlichen Taten, Intrigen und Liebesromanzen zugesehen. Noch heute sind in Deutschlands Landschaften Burgen reich gesät, in denen sich die Magie vergangener Zeiten förmlich spüren lässt. Zu den schönsten unter ihnen gehört sicherlich die Wasserburg Anholt, die in Teilen zu einem Luxushotel umgestaltet wurde. Und sie wirkt tatsächlich so dramatisch, wie man es von einer richtigen Burg erwartet, Wassergraben eingeschlossen. Aber auch innen ist sie nicht minder atemberaubend, denn unter ihren vielen Schätzen befindet sich unter anderem auch eine riesige Kunstsammlung. Alte Meister sind zu Hunderten ausgestellt. Ihrem beeindruckenden Äußeren entspricht die Geschichte der Burg Anholt. Sie widerstand vielen Belagerungen, von denen jene durch Napoleons Truppen als die härteste gilt.

In den letzten Wochen des Zweiten Weltkriegs wurde der Großteil der Burg durch Bombardierungen der Alliierten zerstört. Viele Jahre lang dauerte der Wiederaufbau, der Stein für Stein voranging. Heute sind die weitläufige Bibliothek und die aufwändigen Empfangsräume wieder so prachtvoll wie einst. Und der Folterkeller, der eine Sammlung von Ritterrüstungen beherbergt, ist so gruselig geworden, wie er sein sollte.

Buchtipp: »Geheimes Wissen. Verlorene Techniken der alten Meister« von David Hockney

Au temps des châteaux forts

Les châteaux forts évoquent le passé; que d'histoires ils auraient à raconter si seulement ils pouvaient parler! Leurs murs, donjons et pont-levis ont vu maints chevaliers et rois, en temps de guerre ou de paix, et maints exploits sanglants ou chevaleresques. Sans oublier les intrigues et galanteries de cour ... La campagne allemande est truffée de ces châteaux d'où émane encore la magie des temps passés. L'un des plus beaux est le Wasserburg Anholt, partiellement transformé en hôtel de luxe. Une véritable forteresse médiévale, entourée de douves. Tout aussi impressionnant, l'intérieur renferme une multitude de trésors, dont une vaste collection d'art comprenant des centaines de tableaux de maîtres. L'histoire du château d'Anholt est aussi fabuleuse que son architecture: il a résisté à de nombreux sièges, entre autres l'assaut implacable des armées napoléoniennes.

Une grande partie de l'édifice a été détruite par les bombardements alliés lors de la Deuxième Guerre mondiale. Il a été reconstruit brique par brique pendant de nombreuses années. La bibliothèque et les salles de réception ont retrouvé leur splendeur passée. Le donjon, qui abrite une collection d'armures, n'a rien perdu de son aspect sinistre.

Livre à emporter: « Savoirs secrets: les techniques perdues des maîtres anciens » de David Hockney

ANREISE	Das Schloss liegt nahe der holländischen Grenze, in Isselburg-Anholt, ungefähr 60 km nördlich von Oberhausen und Duisburg
PREIS	Zwischen 95 und 180 €, inklusive Frühstück
ZIMMER	28 Zimmer und Suiten
KÜCHE	Gourmetrestaurant (außer für Folterknechte), etwas bescheidenere Verpflegung in den alten Ställen
GESCHICHTE	Anholt entstand in drei Bauperioden zwischen dem 12. und 17. Jahrhundert. Es wurde 1968 als Hotel eröffnet
X-FAKTOR	Ein wirklich beeindruckendes Schloss mit einer nicht minder beeindruckenden Kunstsammlung

ACCÈS	Le château se trouve à Isselburg-Anholt, près de la frontière hollandaise; à environ 60 km au nord des villes d'Oberhausen et de Duisburg
PRIX	De 95 à 180 €, petit déjeuner compris
CHAMBRES	28 chambres dont plusieurs suites
RESTAURATION	Cuisine gastronomique; restaurant dans les anciennes étables pour les goûts plus modestes
HISTOIRE	Construit pendant trois périodes entre le XIIe et le XVIIe siècle, Anholt a été reconstruit après la Deuxième Guerre mondiale et ouvrait ses portes en 1968
LES « PLUS »	Un vrai château doté d'une prestigieuse collection d'art

Royal antecedents...
Hotel Kaiserin Elisabeth, Bayern

Hotel Kaiserin Elisabeth, Bayern

Royal antecedents

They will put up with imperious conduct here; but only if you can claim to be one of the crowned heads of Europe. There is a proud tradition of royalty in this place.

For 25 years, this is where the Empress of Austria chose to spend her summer holiday. The childhood home of Elisabeth, or Sissi, as she was lovingly called, was near here. After she was married, she often came back to see her family. She was the most famous guest of this 200-year-old inn and did not tire of coming here. And as a large entourage escorted her, she no doubt was the most valued of guests. After her life had been so cruelly put to an end in Geneva, the Hotel Kaiserin Elisabeth was named in her honour. A statue of her is to be found in the gardens. It is placed where she often sat, gazing across the lake towards the foothills of the Alps. The landscape is one of this place's most attractive features; another is the renowned golf course. Those who don't play can stay on the terrace, reading or writing poetry, just as the Empress once did. Going to see the castles built by her cousins, such as King Ludwig II, is one of many other options.

Book to pack: "Death by Fame: A Life of Elisabeth, Empress of Austria" by Andrew Sinclair

Hotel Kaiserin Elisabeth
Tutzinger Straße 2-6
82340 Feldafing
Germany
Tel: + 49 (0) 8157 9309-0
Fax: + 49 (0) 8157 9309-133
E-mail: info@kaiserin-elisabeth.de
Website: www.kaiserin-elisabeth.de

DIRECTIONS	30 km/19 m south of Munich
RATES	From € 97 to 281, including breakfast
ROOMS	65 rooms
FOOD	German and Austrian specialities
HISTORY	Built in the 19th century, the hotel has been enlarged and renovated several times since then
X-FACTOR	The romantic view and history

Adel verpflichtet

Hoheitsvolles Gebaren würde man hier sicherlich dulden.
Allerdings nur, wenn Sie beweisen können, eines der
gekrönten Häupter Europas zu sein. Denn man ist stolz auf
die eigene königliche Tradition.

25 Jahre lang verbrachte Ihre Königliche Hoheit Elisabeth,
Kaiserin von Österreich und Königin von Ungarn, hier ihren
Sommerurlaub. Auch steht das Haus, in dem Sissi, wie sie
meist genannt wurde, aufwuchs, nicht weit von hier; und
nach ihrer Heirat kehrte sie oft hierher zurück, um die
Familie zu besuchen.

Sissi war der berühmteste Gast in diesem 200 Jahre alten
Gasthof. Und da sie mit großem Gefolge anzureisen pflegte,
gehörte sie zweifelsohne auch zu den beliebtesten. Und
Elisabeth schien dieses Orts nicht müde zu werden. Nach
ihrem Tod durch ein Attentat nannte sich das Hotel ihr zu
Ehren Hotel Kaiserin Elisabeth. Im Garten des Hotels wurde
eine Statue von ihr genau an dem Platz aufgestellt, an dem
sie oft saß, um den Blick über den See und auf die Ausläufer
der Alpen zu genießen.

Neben der herrlichen Landschaft ist ein weiterer Anziehungspunkt der berühmte Golfplatz. Wer aber nicht Golf spielt,
kann auf Elisabeths Spuren wandeln, auf der Terrasse
ruhen, lesen oder Gedichte schreiben, genau wie sie damals.
Natürlich gehört auch eine Besichtigung der Schlösser ihres
Cousins, König Ludwigs II. von Bayern, zu den vielen
Freizeitmöglichkeiten.

**Buchtipp: »Elisabeth. Kaiserin wider Willen« von Brigitte
Hamann**

Antécédents royaux

Une attitude impériale sera acceptée à condition que vous
soyez issus d'une famille royale européenne! Car ici, la
tradition impériale perdure. C'est en effet en ce lieu que
l'impératrice d'Autriche vint passer ses vacances d'été pendant quelque vingt-cinq ans. La maison d'enfance d'Élisabeth
– plus connue sous le nom de Sissi – se trouvait juste à côté.
Après son mariage, Sissi revint souvent rendre visite à sa
famille, ne se lassant jamais de cet endroit enchanteur.

Elle était l'hôtesse la plus illustre de l'hôtel bicentenaire et
sans doute la cliente la plus appréciée en raison de la vaste
escorte qui l'accompagnait. Après son assassinat à Genève
l'hôtel fut rebaptisé Kaiserin Elisabeth en son honneur.
Dans le jardin, une statue de l'impératrice se dresse à l'endroit où elle aimait contempler le lac au pied des Alpes.

Le paysage est l'un des grands atouts de l'hôtel, de même
que le terrain de golf très réputé. Ceux qui ne souhaitent pas
jouer peuvent rester sur la terrasse à lire ou à écrire de la
poésie, comme le faisait jadis Sissi. La visite des châteaux
construits par ses cousins, notamment Louis II de Bavière,
compte parmi les nombreuses excursions à faire dans la
région.

**Livre à emporter : « Élisabeth d'Autriche » d'Egon César, comte
Corti**

ANREISE	30 km südlich von München entfernt
PREIS	Zwischen 97 und 281 €, Frühstück inklusive
ZIMMER	65 Zimmer
KÜCHE	Deutsche und österreichische Spezialitäten
GESCHICHTE	Der Gasthof stammt aus dem 19. Jahrhundert und wurde seither mehrmals erweitert und renoviert
X-FAKTOR	Der wunderbare Blick und die romantische Geschichte des Hauses

ACCÈS	À 30 km au sud de Munich
PRIX	De 97 à 281 €, petit déjeuner compris
CHAMBRES	65 chambres
RESTAURATIONS	Spécialités allemandes et autrichiennes
HISTOIRE	Construit au XIXe siècle, l'hôtel a été agrandi et rénové plusieurs fois
LES « PLUS »	Vue romantique et contexte historique

Menüs à la
Kaiserin Elisabeth

Kulinarisches und Lyrisches

Bearbeitet von
Else Bertau und Dieter Ulrich
Herausgegeben von
Eva Freifrau von Gleichenstein

Once upon a time...
Hotel Schlossgut Oberambach, Bayern

Hotel Schlossgut Oberambach, Bayern

Once upon a time

The German state of Bavaria is the home of castles. Especially the ones that were built at the behest of the legendary king, Ludwig II. These look as though they were taken from a fairy-tale setting. Every visitor who comes to see them is overwhelmed. The creators of Disneyland chose the most famous of them all, Neuschwanstein, as the model for their Cinderella Castle, which is the jewel of the Magic Kingdom.

Along the shores of the picturesque Lake Starnberg, there are several enchanting abodes, too. Looking out over the lake, the Hotel Schlossgut Oberambach is a real palace, where guests are made to feel they're a Prince or Princess Charming. You may not be able to live here happily ever after, but when you leave, you will surely feel better. This is a haven of well-being; harmony is the house rule. Everything is planned to return you to your real life rested and on form. The history of the building may go back as far as the 15th century, but the owners are up to date in their ecological consciousness. The hotel has high environmental values; the food that is served is both healthy and delicious; the swimming pool was built in line with the philosophy of Feng Shui.

Book to pack: "Ludwig II of Bavaria: The Swan King" by Christopher McIntosh

Hotel Schlossgut Oberambach
82541 Münsing
Germany
Tel: + 49 (0) 8177 93 23
Fax: + 49 (0) 8177 93 24 00
E-mail: info@schlossgut.de
Website: www.schlossgut.de

DIRECTIONS	Less than an hour's drive southwest of Munich
RATES	From € 115; suites from € 185, breakfast € 15
ROOMS	38 rooms
FOOD	Gourmet organic cuisine
HISTORY	The origins of the Schlossgut lie in the 15th century. The building has been transformed several times over the centuries. It opened as a hotel in 1997.
X-FACTOR	A place to restore body & soul

Es war einmal

Bayernland ist Schlösserland. Besonders die Schlösser, die König Ludwig II. erbauen ließ, scheinen aus einer Märchenkulisse zu stammen. Sie begeisterten unter anderem auch die Schöpfer von Disneyland, die das berühmteste von ihnen, das Schloss Neuschwanstein, kopierten und in Cinderella Castle umtauften. Auch rund um den idyllischen Starnberger See finden sich einige entzückende Anwesen.

Ein echtes Schlösschen mit Seeblick ist das Hotel Schlossgut Oberambach. So erholsam ist es hier, dass der Gast zum Märchenprinzen oder zur Prinzessin wird. Harmonie heißt die Hausregel des Hotels, das so ein wahrer Zufluchtsort des Wohlgefühls ist. Sie werden hier wohl nicht bis an Ihr Lebensende glücklich leben können, doch werden Sie sich nach einem Aufenthalt sicher besser fühlen. Das gesamte Planen und Wirken des Hotels ist darauf ausgerichtet, die Gäste entspannt und aufgetankt wieder ins richtige Leben zu entlassen. Auch wenn die Wurzeln des Hotels im 15. Jahrhundert liegen, so ist doch seine Philosophie ganz modern, besonders was das ökologische Bewusstsein angeht, welches hier als wichtigster Wert gilt. So ist das Essen gesund und dennoch köstlich und der Swimmingpool wurde nach den Grundprinzipien des Feng Shui gestaltet.

Buchtipp: »Der tragische König. Leben und Tod König Ludwigs II. von Bayern« von Erika Brunner

Il était une fois

La Bavière est le pays des châteaux. Ceux construits sous le règne de Louis II de Bavière semblent sortir tout droit de contes de fées. Ils ont notamment séduit les créateurs de Disneyland qui ont copié le plus célèbre d'entre eux – Neuschwanstein – rebaptisé le « Château de Cendrillon ». Mais on peut voir d'autres édifices fabuleux sur les rives du lac de Starnberg.

L'un d'eux est un véritable palais où vous deviendrez princesse ou prince charmant le temps de votre séjour. Havre de paix, l'hôtel Schlossgut Oberambach mise sur le bien-être et l'harmonie. Peut-être n'y vivrez-vous pas heureux jusqu'à la fin de vos jours, mais vous serez sûrement régénéré quand vous le quitterez. Tout y est programmé pour vous rendre reposé et en pleine forme à la vie de tous les jours. Si l'origine du château remonte au XVe siècle, l'hôtel qu'il abrite aujourd'hui est très moderne en matière d'écologie, ce dont témoignent la délicieuse cuisine bioénergétique et la piscine conçue selon les principes du Feng Shui.

Livre à emporter : « Louis II de Bavière » de Pierre Combescot

ANREISE	Eine knappe Autostunde südwestlich von München entfernt
PREIS	Zimmer ab 115 €, Suiten ab 185 €, Frühstück 15 €
ZIMMER	38 Zimmer
KÜCHE	Bio-Küche auf höchstem Niveau
GESCHICHTE	Das Schlossgut geht auf das 15. Jahrhundert zurück. Es wurde in den folgenden Jahrhunderten häufig umgebaut und 1997 als Hotel eröffnet
X-FAKTOR	Ein Ort, an dem Körper und Seele auftanken können

ACCÈS	À moins d'une heure de route au sud-ouest de Munich
PRIX	À partir de 115 €, suites de 185 €, petit déjeuner 15 €
CHAMBRES	38 chambres
RESTAURATION	Excellente cuisine bio
HISTOIRE	L'origine du Schlossgut remonte au XVe siècle. Le bâtiment a été transformé plusieurs fois au cours des siècles et a ouvert ses portes en 1997
LES « PLUS »	Endroit idéal pour revivifier le corps et l'esprit

The red retreat...
Hotel Vila Bled, Bled

Hotel Vila Bled, Bled

The red retreat

In the northwest of Slovenia, nestled in the Julian Alps, is the breathtakingly lovely Lake Bled. Within this romantic fairytale setting, there is a residence with a real political story to tell. Once the summer home of the former Yugoslav royal family, and rebuilt to serve as the country villa of Marshal Tito, the Hotel Vila Bled now welcomes a more egalitarian range of guests within its walls. Despite its mid-1980s conversion to a prestigious hotel, the 1950s architecture and design has been left largely untouched. Much of the furniture, porcelain, and silverware are original, dating from its Eastern-Bloc days. The interior is an intriguing combination of austerity and ornamentation, with polished marble floors inset with colourful mosaics, plain chairs swathed in velvet, and patterned wall-coverings.

From the hotel's balconies and pavilion restaurant, you can look out at the picturesque island, where the little St. Marija Church has stood for centuries. Across the lake is the grim-looking medieval Castle Bled, imposingly sited on a huge rock. Summer or winter, this is a magical place with charismatic scenery and a powerful past.

Books to pack: "Black Lamb and Grey Falcon: A Journey through Yugoslavia" by Rebecca West
"The Radetzky March" by Joseph Roth

Hotel Vila Bled	
Cesta svobode 26	
Sl-4260 Bled	
Slovenia	
Tel: + 386 (0) 45 791 500	
Fax: + 386 (0) 45 741 320	
E-mail: hotel@vila-bled.com	
Website: www.vila-bled.com	

DIRECTIONS	35 km/22 m north from Ljubljana Brnik International Airport, 35 km/22 m south from border crossings with Austria (Karawankentunnel) and 45 km/28 m from Italy (Ratece)
RATES	€ 95 to 360
ROOMS	30 rooms, including suites
FOOD	Slovenian cuisine
HISTORY	Built in 1947 for Marshal Tito, the Hotel Vila Bled opened in 1984
X-FACTOR	Fairytale setting and 1950s communist style

Die rote Zuflucht

Im Nordwesten Sloweniens, mitten in den Julianischen Alpen, liegt der atemberaubend schöne See von Bled. An diesem märchenhaft romantischen Fleckchen Erde befindet sich ein Domizil mit überaus spannender politischer Geschichte. Das Hotel Vila Bled diente früher der jugoslawischen Königsfamilie als Sommerresidenz und wurde später zum Landsitz von Präsident Tito umgebaut. Heute beherbergen seine Mauern jedoch Gäste aller Art. Beim Umbau des Gebäudes Mitte der 1980er-Jahre zu einem Luxushotel erhielt man zum größten Teil die Architektur und das Design aus den 1950er-Jahren. Auch zahlreiche Möbel sowie das Porzellan und das Silberbesteck stammen noch aus der Ostblock-Ära. Die Interieurs zeigen eine faszinierende Kombination aus Schlichtheit und Prunk, die in polierten Marmorböden mit farbigen Mosaiken ebenso zum Ausdruck kommt wie in gemusterten Tapeten und einfachen Stühlen, die mit luxuriösem Samt bezogen sind.

Von den Balkonen und dem Restaurantpavillon des Hotels aus blicken Sie auf eine malerische Insel, auf der die kleine, jahrhundertealte Kirche St. Marija steht. Am anderen Ufer des Sees thront die trutzige mittelalterliche Burg Bled auf einem hohen Felsen. Dieser magische Ort mit seiner eindrucksvollen Vergangenheit und faszinierenden Landschaft ist im Sommer wie im Winter ein besonderes Erlebnis.

Buchtipps: »Black Lamb and Grey Falcon. A Journey through Yugoslavia« von Rebecca West
»Radetzkymarsch« von Joseph Roth

Un refuge rouge

Au nord-ouest de la Slovénie, dans les Alpes Juliennes, s'étend le lac Bled, d'une beauté à couper le souffle. Ce cadre de conte de fées abrite une résidence dont les murs, s'ils parlaient, pourraient relater l'histoire politique des lieux. Villégiature d'été de la famille royale de Yougoslavie, reconstruit ensuite pour le maréchal Tito auquel il servit de maison de campagne, le Vila Bled fait désormais preuve d'un plus grand égalitarisme quant aux hôtes qu'il accueille. Transformé en un hôtel prestigieux au milieu des années 1980, il conserve toutefois son architecture et son style des années 1950. Le mobilier, la porcelaine et l'argenterie sont en bonne partie d'origine et datent de la période communiste. L'intérieur est un étonnant mélange d'austérité et d'ornementation : sols en marbre poli incrustés de mosaïques multicolores, sièges tout simples revêtus de velours et riches tentures murales.

Des balcons et du restaurant-pavillon de l'hôtel, on a vue sur une île pittoresque où la petite église Sainte-Marija se dresse depuis des siècles. Sur l'autre rive du lac, le château médiéval de Bled, d'aspect sinistre, couronne un énorme rocher. Été comme hiver, c'est un lieu magique empreint d'histoire, au paysage extraordinaire.

Livres à emporter : « Agneau noir et Faucon gris : un voyage à travers la Yougoslavie » de Rebecca West
« La Marche de Radetzky » de Joseph Roth

ANREISE	35 km nördlich vom internationalen Flughafen Brnik in Ljubljana, 35 km südlich von der österreichischen Grenze (Karawankentunnel) und 45 km von Italien (Grenzübergang Ratece)
PREIS	Zwischen 95 und 360 €
ZIMMER	30, einschließlich Suiten
KÜCHE	Slowenische Küche
GESCHICHTE	1947 für Präsident Tito erbaut, als Hotel Vila Bled 1984 eröffnet
X-FAKTOR	Märchenhafte Lage und sozialistisches Design der 1950er-Jahre

ACCÈS	À 35 km au nord de l'aéroport international Brnik de Ljubljana, à 35 km au sud de la frontière avec l'Autriche (Karawankentunnel) et à 45 km de l'Italie (Ratece)
PRIX	De 95 à 360 €
CHAMBRES	30 chambres et suites
RESTAURATION	Cuisine slovène
HISTOIRE	Construit en 1947 pour le maréchal Tito, le Vila Bled a ouvert ses portes en 1984
LES « PLUS »	Cadre de conte de fées et style des années 1950

Nature, no ornament...
Hotel Alpenhof Kreuzberg Looshaus, Payerbach

Hotel Alpenhof Kreuzberg
Looshaus, Payerbach

Nature, no ornament

"Design a country house for me; rustic, but with style", might have been the brief that Paul Khuner gave the famous architect Adolf Loos.

This is the house that was built for him in 1930. Loos was keen on design that was free of decoration, and explained his beliefs in an essay titled "Ornament and Crime". He argued that rich materials and good workmanship made up for a lack of decoration, and in fact far outshone it. The house may not be a decorative one, but it is not plain. Kept preserved much like it was when first built, it is now a hotel. The Alpenhof Kreuzberg Looshaus is perched high on a hillside in the Austrian Alps, encircled by fresh clean mountain air. While its function has altered, the present owners have guarded its original nature, which is as it should be for a building that has been recognized as a state treasure. Although some renovation has been carried out, it is in accord with the design. The colourful interior is proof of the architect's edict that planning should be done from the inside out, and his fondness for cubic shapes is obvious. The region is famed for its winter sports and spas, as well as being home to this design jewel.

Books to pack: "Ornament and Crime" by Adolf Loos
"Brother of Sleep" by Robert Schneider

Hotel Alpenhof Kreuzberg Looshaus		
Kreuzberg 60	DIRECTIONS	An hour's drive south of Vienna
2650 Payerbach	RATES	€ 24 to 34, breakfast included
Austria	ROOMS	14 rooms
Tel: + 43 (0) 2666 52911	FOOD	Renowned home-style cooking with regional specialities
Fax: + 43 (0) 2666 5291134		
E-mail: steiner@looshaus.at	HISTORY	Built in 1930, the Looshaus was adapted as a holiday resort at the beginning of the 1950s
Website: www.looshaus.at	X-FACTOR	Design classic in a spectacular setting

Natur, keine Ornamente

»Entwerfen Sie mir ein Landhaus, rustikal, aber mit Stil«, so mag die Anweisung des Lebensmittelfabrikanten Paul Khuner an den berühmten Architekten Adolf Loos gelautet haben.

Das Ergebnis ist dieses 1930 erbaute Haus. Loos war Verfechter eines geradlinigen, schnörkellosen Stils, der seine Philosophie in einem Essay mit dem viel sagenden Titel »Ornament und Verbrechen« erläuterte. Seiner Meinung nach waren hochwertige Materialien und handwerkliches Können weitaus wichtiger als dekorative Elemente. Und so ist dieses zweigeschossige Blockhaus, das bei seiner Umgestaltung zu dem heutigen Hotel weitgehend im Originalzustand belassen wurde, auch nicht überschwäng-lich ausgeschmückt, dabei jedoch alles andere als schlicht. Das Hotel Alpenhof Kreuzberg Looshaus liegt an einem Berghang hoch in den österreichischen Alpen, umgeben von frischer, reiner Bergluft. Obwohl es seine Funktion geändert hat, haben die heutigen Besitzern es originalgetreu renoviert, wie es einem Gebäude angemessen ist, das als nationales Baudenkmal anerkannt wurde. Notwendige Renovierungs-arbeiten erfolgten in engem Einklang mit dem ursprüng-lichen Design. Die farbenfrohen Interieurs sind der beste Beweis dafür, dass ein Haus von innen nach außen geplant werden sollte, so wie es der Architekt forderte, und zeugen von seiner Liebe zu kubischen Formen.

Abgesehen von diesem architektonischen Juwel ist die Region berühmt für ihr Wintersportangebot und ihre Kurorte.

Buchtipps: »Ornament und Verbrechen« von Adolf Loos
»Schlafes Bruder« von Robert Schneider

Nature sans ornements

« Dessinez-moi une maison de campagne, rustique, mais qui ait du style! » Telle aurait pu être la commande passée par Paul Khuner au célèbre architecte Adolf Loos, et telle est la maison construite pour lui en 1930.

Loos préconisait une architecture dépouillée et a exposé ses principes dans un manifeste intitulé « Ornement et Crime ». Il affirmait que la richesse des matériaux et la qualité du travail compensaient l'absence de décoration, qu'en fait, ces deux facteurs jouaient un rôle bien plus important. Si la maison n'est pas décorative, elle sort cependant de l'ordinaire. Transformée en hôtel, elle conserve en grande partie son état d'origine.

L'Alpenhof Kreuzberg Looshaus, perché à flanc de montagne dans les Alpes autrichiennes, respire l'air frais alpin. Bien qu'il ait changé de fonction, devenant hôtel, ses propriétaires actuels ont veillé à lui garder son aspect original, comme il se doit pour un bâtiment classé. Les quelques rénovations effectuées s'accordent avec la conception d'origine. L'aména-gement aux couleurs vives illustre parfaitement la prédilection de l'architecte pour les formes cubiques et son principe selon lequel la conception devait se faire de l'intérieur.

Outre pour ce bijou d'architecture, la région est réputée pour ses stations de sports d'hiver et ses villes d'eau.

Livre à emporter : « Frère sommeil » de Robert Schneider

ANREISE	Eine Fahrstunde mit dem Auto südlich von Wien
PREIS	Zwischen 24 und 34 €, Frühstück inklusive
ZIMMER	14 Zimmer
KÜCHE	Berühmte Hausmannskost mit regionalen Spezialitäten
GESCHICHTE	1930 erbaut und Anfang der 1950er-Jahre zum Hotel umgebaut
X-FAKTOR	Design-Klassiker in spektakulärer Umgebung

ACCÈS	À une heure de route au sud de Vienne
PRIX	De 24 à 34 €, petit déjeuner compris
CHAMBRES	14 chambres
RESTAURATION	Cuisine familiale réputée avec spécialités régionales
HISTOIRE	Construit en 1930, le Looshaus a été transformé en hôtel au début des années 1950
LES « PLUS »	Design classique dans un cadre spectaculaire

End of the road...
Hotel Belvédère, Wengeń

Hotel Belvédère, Wengen

End of the road

No road leads here. The only way to reach this Swiss village is by mountain railway. However, there are some who won't be disheartened by this fact. If you are here in September, you can watch them run into town; as competitors in what must be one of the most gruelling marathons in the world. The runners pass through Wengen, on their way to even greater heights. In January, athletes in the Downhill Ski Racing World Cup head the opposite way.

Those of us who are not in such a hurry can stay put at the Belvédère Hotel. Rather than run up or ski down the mountains, you can look out at them from the balconies. The charming hotel was built in 1912, and has been kept in its *art nouveau* style. It is in the centre of the lively village, and skiing, hiking, and mountaineering routes are all easily accessible.

As well as the great views, the advantage of the place is that there is little time wasted before setting ski to snow. This is a perfect starting point for several ski runs, most of which lead back to the village; as well as miles of ski pistes there are paths for walkers, and cable cars that take passengers to other picturesque villages.

Book to pack: "The Magic Mountain" by Thomas Mann

Hotel Belvédère	
Familie Zinnert	
3823 Wengen	
Switzerland	
Tel: + 41 (0) 33 856 68 68	
Fax: + 41 (0) 33 856 68 69	
E-mail: belvedere@belvedere-wengen.ch	
Website: www.belvedere-wengen.ch	

DIRECTIONS	Wengen is about 70 km south of Bern. From Interlaken by rail to Lauterbrunnen and then to Wengen. The hotel is five minutes walk from the Wengen train station
RATES	From € 49 to 80, including breakfast
ROOMS	62 rooms
FOOD	Bracing classic Swiss fare served in the hotel's restaurant. Nearby is the Piz Gloria, a revolving restaurant 3,000 m up, on the top of one of the highest peaks in Europe
HISTORY	The Belvédère was built 1912 in the *art nouveau* style
X-FACTOR	Character hotel in a resort village that have both kept their charm

Am Ende der Straße

Es gibt keine Straße, sondern nur eine Bergbahn, mit der Sie dieses schweizerische Dorf erreichen können. Doch einige Leute scheinen diese Tatsache zu ignorieren. Im September kann man ihnen dabei zusehen, wie sie in die Stadt rennen, genauer gesagt, wie sie an einem der anstrengendsten Marathonläufe der Welt teilnehmen. Die Läufer passieren Wengen, bevor sie noch größere Höhen erklimmen müssen. Im Januar aber rasen die Sportler beim World Cup im Abfahrtslauf in genau die entgegengesetzte Richtung. Wer jedoch keine solche Eile hat, kann einfach im Hotel Belvédère bleiben. Anstatt die Berge hinaufzurennen oder herabzudonnern, kann man sie vom Balkon aus einfach nur genießen. Das charmante Hotel stammt aus dem Jahr 1912; seine Jugendstil-Architektur wurde bis heute erhalten. Mitten im Zentrum des äußerst lebendigen Skiortes gelegen, lässt es sich direkt vor der Haustür natürlich auch Ski fahren, wandern oder bergsteigen.

Abgesehen vom wunderschönen Panorama hat Wengen noch einen anderen großen Pluspunkt. Skiläufer müssen keine langen Wege auf sich nehmen, sondern gelangen schnell zu mehreren Pisten, von denen die meisten ins Dorf zurückführen. Außerdem gibt es Wanderwege sowie Gondeln, die sie zu anderen, nicht minder pittoresken Dörfern und wieder zurückbringen.

Buchtipp: »Der Zauberberg« von Thomas Mann

Le bout du monde

Il n'y a pas de route pour s'y rendre; seul un petit train de montagne permet d'accéder à ce village suisse. Mais certains ne l'utilisent même pas : si vous séjournez ici en septembre, vous verrez une foule pressée avancer vers la ville, dans le cadre de ce qui doit être l'un des plus rudes marathons du monde. Les coureurs traversent Wengen avant de s'élancer dans les hauteurs. En janvier, les athlètes de la Coupe du monde de ski alpin dévalent dans l'autre sens.

Les moins sportifs, quant à eux, choisiront de loger à l'Hôtel Belvédère. Plutôt que de gravir les montagnes ou les descendre à ski, ils observeront les champions depuis leur balcon. Ce charmant hôtel de style Art nouveau, construit en 1912, est situé au centre du village animé. Il se prête à toutes les activités de montagne, ski, randonnée et alpinisme.

Outre un superbe panorama, le Belvédère offre un accès direct aux pistes de ski, dont la plupart rejoignent le village. En plus des kilomètres de pistes, on trouvera également de beaux sentiers de randonnée et des téléphériques menant à d'autres localités pittoresques des environs.

Livre à emporter : « La Montagne magique » de Thomas Mann

ANREISE	Wengen liegt etwa 70 km südlich von Bern. Mit dem Zug erreichen Sie Wengen von Interlaken über Lauterbrunnen. Vom Bahnhof sind es nur fünf Minuten zu Fuß zum Hotel
PREIS	Zwischen 49 und 80 €, Frühstück inklusive
ZIMMER	62 Zimmer
KÜCHE	Klassische schweizerische Küche im Hotelrestaurant. In der Nähe liegt in 3000 m Höhe, auf einem der höchsten Gipfel Europas, das Drehrestaurant Piz Gloria
GESCHICHTE	Das Belvédère wurde 1912 im Jugendstil erbaut
X-FAKTOR	Individuelles Hotel in einem Erholungsort – beide mit großem Charme

ACCÈS	À environ 70 km au sud de Berne. En train depuis Interlaken via Lauterbrunnen ; l'hôtel est à 5 minutes à pied de la gare de Wengen
PRIX	De 49 à 80 €, petit déjeuner compris
CHAMBRES	62 chambres
RESTAURATION	Le restaurant de l'hôtel sert de solides spécialités suisses. À proximité, le Piz Gloria est un restaurant panoramique situé à 3000 m d'altitude
HISTOIRE	L'hôtel de style Art nouveau a été construit en 1912
LES « PLUS »	Hôtel de caractère dans une station de sports d'hiver de charme

On top of the world...
Badrutt's Palace Hotel, St. Moritz

Badrutt's Palace Hotel, St. Moritz

On top of the world

This grand old hotel is as much a symbol of St. Moritz as are the mountains and the lake. In the late 19th century, the original owners are credited with creating what were then brand new winter sports. Before that time, travellers came to the Alps much more in summer; to hike across the hillsides, see the wildflowers and the massive peaks. By building the world's first toboggan run, and a curling rink, the proprietor lured guests to stay at his hotel in the midst of cold weather. The Palace Hotel, with its tower and memorable silhouette, has become a landmark building. Set in splendid and still unspoiled scenery, bounded by private gardens, this is an institution in the best sense of the word. Life is peaceful here, in spite of being at the centre of this highly social resort. Skiing, polo, and horse races on the snow are part of its appeal, as is the climate. St. Moritz boasts that the sun shines here on an average of 322 days a year. In fact, the town's style and name became one so well-liked that it has been registered as a trademark. The brand 'St. Moritz; top of the world' sums up both its location and its status.

Book to pack: "Into Thin Air: A Personal Account of the Mount Everest Disaster" by Jon Krakauer

Badrutt's Palace Hotel	
Via Serlas 27	
7500 St. Moritz	
Switzerland	
Tel: + 41 (0) 81 837 10 00	
Fax: + 41 (0) 81 837 29 99	
E-mail: reservations.palace@	
rosewoodhotels.com	
Website: www.badruttspalace.com	

DIRECTIONS	220 km/137 m southeast from Zurich. The train route through the Grisons to the Engadine is one of the most interesting and picturesque routes of Europe
RATES	From € 234 to 2,892; including breakfast
ROOMS	248; including suites. Closes briefly from Sepember 29 to December 6
FOOD	Three restaurants at the hotel, including a renowned French dining room
HISTORY	The 19th century building opened as the Palace Hotel in 1896
X-FACTOR	The activity on offer – one of the more daring diversions is the Cresta Run, the famous bobsled course

Auf Berges Spitze

Dieses wunderbare alte Grandhotel ist ein Symbol für
St. Moritz genauso wie die Berge und der See. Den ersten
Besitzern wird zugeschrieben, im ausgehenden 19. Jahrhundert den damals völlig neuen Wintersport eingeführt zu
haben. Vorher kamen die Reisenden eher im Sommer in die
Alpen, wanderten, suchten nach wild wachsenden Blumen
und genossen den Anblick der riesigen Bergspitzen. Durch
den Bau der ersten Rodelbahn und einer Curlinganlage ge-
lang es, die Gäste auch im tiefsten Winter und bei niedrigs-
ten Temperaturen zu einem Aufenthalt zu verführen. Heute
ist das Palace Hotel mit seinem Turm und seiner denkwür-
digen Silhouette zu einem Wahrzeichen geworden. In einer
atemberaubenden und bis heute unzerstörten Idylle liegend,
eingesäumt von Privatgärten, ist das Hotel eine Institution,
hinter deren Mauern man sich gerne verstecken mag. Im
Gegensatz zum Trubel von St. Moritz verläuft das Leben
hier friedlich. Skifahren, Polospielen und Pferderennen
im Schnee sind die Hauptattraktionen, vom Klima ganz
abgesehen. Denn St. Moritz ist mit durchschnittlich 322
Sonnentagen im Jahr gesegnet. Stil und Name des Ortes
sind so bekannt und beliebt, dass es mittlerweile ein einge-
tragenes Markenzeichen gibt. Die Marke »St. Moritz – Top
of the World« bezieht sich dabei nicht nur auf die geogra-
fische Lage, sondern auch auf den Status dieses Ortes.
**Buchtipp: »In eisige Höhen. Das Drama am Mount Everest«
von Jon Krakauer**

Au sommet du monde

Ce vieil hôtel magnifique est un symbole de Saint-Moritz
autant que le lac et les montagnes qui entourent la localité.
À la fin du XIXe siècle, ses premiers propriétaires jouèrent
un rôle primordial dans la création des sports d'hiver.
Jusqu'alors, on villégiaturait surtout en été dans les Alpes,
pour y faire de la randonnée, admirer les fleurs sauvages et
les imposants sommets. En construisant la première piste
de luge du monde, ainsi qu'un terrain de curling, l'hôtelier
attira des clients en plein cœur de l'hiver. Le Palace Hotel,
avec sa tour et sa silhouette unique, est devenu un véritable
monument. Situé dans un cadre aussi splendide qu'intact,
et entouré de jardins privés, l'hôtel est une véritable institution, au sens noble du terme. La vie y est paisible, malgré sa
situation en plein centre de cette station très courue. Ski,
polo et courses de chevaux sur la neige font partie de ses
atouts, sans oublier le climat : Saint-Moritz bénéficierait de
322 jours de soleil par an. La station est si renommée que
son nom est devenu une marque déposée. « Saint-Moritz, top
of the world » résume à la fois sa situation et son standing.
Livre à emporter : « Tragédie à l'Everest » de Jon Krakauer

ANREISE	220 km südöstlich von Zürich entfernt. Die Fahrt durch Graubünden und das Engadin gehört zu den malerischsten und interessanten Routen Europas
PREIS	Zwischen 234 und 2892 €, Frühstück inklusive
ZIMMER	248 Zimmer, Suiten eingeschlossen. Vom 29. September bis zum 6. Dezember ist das Hotel geschlossen
KÜCHE	Das Hotel verfügt über drei Restaurants, darunter einen berühmten Dinersaal im französischen Stil
GESCHICHTE	Das Hotel aus dem 19. Jahrhundert eröffnete 1896
X-FAKTOR	Das Angebot an Aktivitäten. Für den Cresta-Run auf der gleichnamigen Bob-Bahn muss man etwas Mut aufbringen

ACCÈS	À 220 km au sud-est de Zurich. La ligne de chemin de fer à destination d'Engadine, qui traverse les Grisons, est l'un des trajets les plus pittoresques d'Europe
PRIX	De 234 à 2892 €, petit déjeuner compris
CHAMBRES	248 chambres, dont plusieurs suites. Fermeture annuelle du 29 septembre au 6 décembre
RESTAURATION	L'hôtel compte trois restaurants, dont le restaurant français, très réputé
HISTOIRE	Construit au XIXe siècle, l'hôtel a ouvert ses portes en 1896
LES « PLUS »	Les activités proposées, notamment le Cresta Run, célèbre course de bobsleigh

Majestic seclusion...
Château de Bagnols, Bourgogne

Château de Bagnols, Bourgogne

Majestic seclusion

Lord of all you can see – at least this could be your dream, as you look out from the ramparts of what was once a fortress, and now is a secluded retreat.

Complete with moat and drawbridge, the Château de Bagnols stands on a high vantage point in the lovely Burgundy country-side, guarding its guests from the public gaze and cares of the outside world. Hidden behind massive stone buttresses and towers are a fabulous hotel and garden, a haven for the fortunate few. First built in 1221 as a medieval stronghold, the Chateau is now one of France's historic monuments, restored to its rightful splendour. Its portcullis opens to reveal peaceful gardens and terraces, sheltered by yew hedges and encircled by a stone wall. After entering the castle's courtyard, the arriving guests step into an atmosphere of history and grandeur. Many of the rooms have striking Renaissance wall paintings, uncovered during recent restoration. Antique beds are hung with period silk velvets and embroideries; rich tapestries adorn walls, and great elaborately carved fireplaces blaze out warmth in the winter.

The famous vineyards of Beaujolais and the charming towns and villages in the rolling green hills and valleys beyond may well tempt you out from your castle realm.

Book to pack: "The Red and the Black" by Stendhal

Château de Bagnols

69620 Bagnols
France
Tel: + 33 (0) 474 71 4000
Fax: + 33 (0) 474 71 4049
E-mail: 100446.1654@compuserve.com
Website: www.bagnols.com

DIRECTIONS	24 km/15 m north of Lyon
RATES	€ 397 to 1145; open April to January, or by arrangement
ROOMS	20 rooms, including 8 apartments
FOOD	Beaujolais cuisine, regional specialities
HISTORY	Built in 1221, the château has been transformed several times over the centuries. The hotel was opened in 1991
X-FACTOR	Regal rural retreat, privacy assured

Majestätische Ruhe

Wenn Sie vom Schutzwall dieser ehemaligen Festung um sich schauen, werden Sie sich wie der Herr über die Ihnen zu Füßen liegenden Ländereien fühlen. Denn das Château de Bagnols, umgeben von einem Graben mit einer Ziehbrücke, überragt majestätisch die liebliche Landschaft des Burgund. Heute birgt es ein abgeschiedenes Plätzchen, das Schutz vor der Außenwelt bietet.

Versteckt hinter massiven steinernen Pfeilern und Türmen befindet sich ein Hotel mit einem wunderschönen Garten, in dem Sie sich herrlich entspannen können. Das im Jahr 1221 errichtete mittelalterliche Château gehört heute zu Frankreichs Baudenkmälern. Hinter seinem Falltor erstrecken sich friedliche Gärten und Terrassen, geschützt durch Eibenhecken und eine steinerne Mauer. Sobald Sie den Burghof betreten, werden Sie von der ganz besonderen Atmosphäre verzaubert. Viele der Zimmer bestechen durch eindrucksvolle Wandgemälde aus der Renaissance, die erst vor kurzem freigelegt wurden. Seidensamtvorhänge und Stickereien zieren die antiken Betten; die Wände sind mit üppigen Gobelins behängt, und große Kamine mit kunstvollen Einfassungen verbreiten im Winter wohlige Wärme.

Doch die berühmten Weinberge des Beaujolais sowie die reizenden Städte und Dörfer, die verstreut über die umgebenden Hügel und Täler liegen, sind geschaffen dafür, Sie auch gelegentlich hinter Ihren Burgmauern hervorzulocken.

Buchtipp: »Rot und Schwarz« von Stendhal

Une retraite majestueuse

Montez sur les remparts de cet ancien château fort, aujourd'hui paisible retraite, et imaginez-vous seigneur des lieux qui s'étendent sous votre regard.

Avec ses douves et son pont-levis, le Château de Bagnols, érigé dans une situation admirable, domine la ravissante campagne bourguignonne. Derrière ses tours et contreforts massifs se cachent un hôtel fabuleux et un charmant parc, paradis pour les happy few. Forteresse médiévale dont la construction débute en 1221, ce château classé monument historique a retrouvé sa splendeur d'antan. La herse se lève pour révéler des jardins et terrasses paisibles, abrités derrière des haies d'ifs et entourés d'un mur en pierre. Histoire et splendeur accueillent les hôtes dès leur arrivée dans la cour du château. Un grand nombre des salles sont revêtues de magnifiques fresques Renaissance, découvertes durant la récente restauration. Les lits anciens sont fermés par des rideaux de velours de soie et de dentelles d'époque ; de riches tapisseries ornent les murs et, en hiver, les grandes cheminées sculptées avec art font rayonner leur chaleur.

Les célèbres vignobles du Beaujolais ainsi que les jolis bourgs et villages qui émaillent ce paysage de collines et vallées verdoyantes vous inciteront certainement à quitter les murs de votre château de rêve.

Livre à emporter : « Le Rouge et le Noir » de Stendhal

ANREISE	24 km nördlich von Lyon		ACCÈS	À 24 km au nord de Lyon
PREIS	Zwischen 397 und 1145 €; Öffnungszeiten April bis Januar oder nach Vereinbarung		PRIX	De 397 à 1145 €, ouvert d'avril à janvier, ou sur demande
ZIMMER	20 Zimmer, einschließlich 8 Apartments		CHAMBRES	20 chambres, dont 8 suites
KÜCHE	Regionale Spezialitäten aus dem Beaujolais		RESTAURATION	Cuisine du Beaujolais, spécialités régionales
GESCHICHTE	Das Gebäude wurde 1221 errichtet und über die Jahrhunderte mehrfach umgebaut. Als Hotel wurde es 1991 eröffnet		HISTOIRE	Construit en 1221, le bâtiment a été transformé plusieurs fois au cours des siècles. L'hôtel a ouvert en 1991
X-FAKTOR	Königliches, ländliches Refugium mit garantiertem Schutz der Privatsphäre		LES « PLUS »	Retraite rurale royale, tranquillité garantie

Where the truffle nose come

Le Chaufourg en Périgord, Dordogne

rom…

Le Chaufourg en Périgord, Dordogne

Where the truffle nose comes from

In the ninth century, the Vikings sailed up the River Dordogne near here, raiding many towns on the way. If this house had already been there, no doubt they would have moved in and stayed put.

It was another eight hundred years before Le Chaufourg was built; its doors are open now to guests seeking peace.

Though it is in the heart of the Dordogne, once you are inside the gates that lead to the courtyard, you have a sense of seclusion from the real world. The quite fairytale façade of the house adds to that feeling. Its white-shuttered doors and ivy-laced windows suggest that there is a charming interior to be revealed; one that will more than match up with the outside. That wish comes true. All the rooms are simply romantic; indeed so much so that you might feel inspired to live here happily ever after.

As well as Vikings, others with a nose for good things have come here. This region is the home of the black truffles, "black pearls" that trained dogs can smell and dig out of the ground. And Cyrano, the owner of the most famous nose of all, was from the nearby town of Bergerac.

Book to pack: "Cyrano de Bergerac" by Edmond Rostand

Le Chaufourg en Périgord

24400 Sourzac-Mussidan
Dordogne
France
Tel: + 33 (0) 5.53.81.01.56
Fax: + 33 (0) 5.53.82.94.87
E-mail:chaufourg.hotel@wanadoo.fr
No website

DIRECTIONS	1.5 hours' drive east from Bordeaux; 26 km/16 m from Bergerac
RATES	€ 136 to 274, 2-night minimum. Open March to November and on reservation
ROOMS	5 rooms and 4 suites
FOOD	A restaurant serving delicious local specialties
HISTORY	Built in the 17th century, Le Chaufourg opened as a hotel in 1991
X-FACTOR	A place to make-believe could be your own

Auf Trüffelsuche

Im 9. Jahrhundert segelten die Wikinger den nahe gelegenen Fluss hinauf und brandschatzten viele Städte auf ihrem Weg. Hätte dieses Haus damals schon gestanden, wären sie sicher stattdessen dort eingezogen und lebten bis heute hier. Doch Le Chaufourg wurde erst acht Jahrhunderte später erbaut, und seine Türen stehen heute friedlicheren Gästen offen. Sobald man die Tore durchschritten hat, die auf den Innenhof des Hotels führen, fühlt man sich vom wirklichen Leben abgeschottet. Fast wie im Märchenland sieht die Fassade des Hauses aus, und die weiß gestrichenen Türen und Läden, die efeuumrankten Fenster lassen ahnen, dass das Innere des Hauses ebenfalls viel Charme besitzt, vielleicht sogar noch mehr. Und die erste Ahnung wird nicht enttäuscht. Alle Zimmer sind sehr romantisch und lassen den Wunsch aufkommen, hier glücklich und zufrieden bis ans Ende der Tage zu leben.
Neben den Wikingern hielten auch andere Lebewesen mit einem »Riecher« für Gutes und Teures hier Einzug. Denn diese Region ist Heimat der schwarzen Trüffel, des »schwarzen Goldes«, das von Trüffelhunden über die Nase aufgenommen und mit den Pfoten aus dem Boden gegraben wird. Auch der Inhaber der berühmtesten Nase der Welt, Cyrano von Bergerac, stammte hier aus der Nähe.
Buchtipp: »Cyrano von Bergerac« von Edmond Rostand

Au pays des truffes

Au IXe siècle, les Vikings remontèrent la rivière toute proche, attaquant de nombreuses localités au passage. Si cette maison avait été là, ils y auraient certainement élu domicile et l'on n'aurait plus entendu parler d'eux.
Mais Le Chaufourg ne fut construit que huit siècles plus tard. Aujourd'hui, il ouvre ses portes à quiconque recherche la tranquillité. Bien que situé en plein cœur de la Dordogne, l'hôtel semble être à des milliers de kilomètres de toute civilisation. Caché au fond d'une cour, il évoque une maison de contes de fées. La façade aux volets blancs et aux fenêtres couronnées de lierre laisse deviner un intérieur plein de cachet et de charme. De fait, toutes les pièces sont si délicieusement romantiques que vous souhaiterez y vivre heureux jusqu'à la fin de vos jours, comme dans les contes. Outre les Vikings, bien d'autres, ayant le nez fin, sont venus en ces lieux. La région est réputée pour ses truffes noires que des chiens dressés détectent et déterrent. Par ailleurs, celui qui était doté du nez le plus célèbre au monde, Cyrano de Bergerac, est originaire de la ville toute proche.
Livre à emporter : « Cyrano de Bergerac » d'Edmond Rostand

ANREISE	1,5 Fahrstunden östlich von Bordeaux, 26 km von Bergerac entfernt
PREIS	Zwischen 136 und 274 €, zwei Nächte Minimum. Geöffnet von März bis November
ZIMMER	5 Zimmer und 4 Suiten
KÜCHE	Ein angeschlossenes Restaurant serviert köstlichste regionale Spezialitäten
GESCHICHTE	Erbaut im 17. Jahrhundert, seit 1991 Hotel
X-FAKTOR	Ein Ort, den man sich wünscht zu besitzen

ACCÈS	À 1,5 heures à l'est de Bordeaux et 26 km de Bergerac
PRIX	De 136 à 274 €, 2 nuits minimum. Ouvert de mars à novembre
CHAMBRES	5 chambres, 4 suites
RESTAURATION	Délicieuses spécialités locales
HISTOIRE	Construit au XVIIe siècle, hôtel depuis 1991
LES « PLUS »	Un endroit où l'on se sent chez soi

In vino veritas
Les Sources de Caudalie, Bordeaux-Martillac

Les Sources de Caudalie, Bordeaux-Martillac

In vino veritas

Wine is good for your health, so doctors say. Here's a hotel where not only can you treat yourself to a glass or two of red or white, you can also bathe in it.

Les Sources de Caudalie is a very palatable hotel; one with special healthcare grafted onto it, and placed most fortuitously in the midst of a vineyard. Whilst being nurtured in the unique *vinothérapie* spa, you can try a Merlot wrap, a Sauvignon massage, or a Crushed Cabernet scrub; some of the anti-ageing and slimming treatments created around grape-based products that could taste as good as they look. There are two restaurants for the gastronome, with a cellar of 15,000 bottles of wine to select from. After dinner, the resolute smoker can retire to a book-lined tower room and join the Cigar-Tasting Club. Others can spoil their taste buds by sampling the vintages in the French Paradox bar.

When you are not pampering yourself in the restaurant or the spa, you can visit neighbouring *grand cru* chateaux by bicycle or limousine, and estates in the Médoc, Sauternes, Pomerol, and Saint-Émilion regions. And when you leave, you can take home bottles of local wines as well as jars of Caudalie's grape skincare.

Book to pack: "Le Grand Meaulnes" by Alain-Fournier

Les Sources de Caudalie	
Chemin de Smith Haut-Lafitte	
33650 Bordeaux-Martillac	
France	
Tel: + 33 (0) 557 838 383	
Fax: + 33 (0) 557 838 384	
E-mail: sources@sources-caudalie.com	
Website: www.sources-caudalie.com	

DIRECTIONS	15 minutes south from Bordeaux
RATES	Rooms from € 175 to 240, suites from € 290 to 425; depending on the season
ROOMS	49 rooms and suites
FOOD	A veritable feast for the senses awaits you
HISTORY	Les Sources de Caudalie were built and opened in 1999
X-FACTOR	Wine treats for palate, senses and body

Im Wein liegt Wahrheit

Ein Gläschen Wein, so sagt der Hausarzt, sei gut für die Gesundheit. Nun, hier können Sie nicht nur einen guten Rot- oder Weißwein trinken, Sie können auch in ihm baden. Les Sources de Caudalie ist ein Hotel, das rundherum dem Gaumen schmeichelt. Nicht nur, dass dieses Hotel eine außergewöhnliche Wellnessanlage besitzt, es liegt zudem zufälligerweise mitten in einem Weinberg.

Wer sich mit der einzigartigen »Vinotherapie« verwöhnen lassen möchte, kann einen Merlotwickel versuchen, eine Sauvignonmassage oder ein Körperpeeling mit zerstoßenen Cabernettraubenkernen. Einige der Behandlungen, ob Anti-Age oder Abnehmkur, basieren auf Weinprodukten und schmecken so gut, wie sie aussehen. Überdies werden dem Feinschmecker gleich zwei Restaurants und ein Weinkeller mit über 15 000 Flaschen geboten. Hartnäckige Raucher dürfen sich nach dem Dinner in die Bibliothek des Turmzimmers zurückziehen und Mitglied des Zigarrenverkostungsclubs werden. Andere verwöhnen in der Bar French Paradox ihre Geschmacksnerven mit Kostproben besonderer Jahrgänge.

Und wenn Sie nicht gerade das Restaurant oder den Wellnessbereich genießen, können Sie zum Beispiel Touren per Fahrrad oder Limousine zu den nahe gelegenen bedeutenden Weingütern der Regionen des Médoc, Sauternes, Pomerol und Saint-Émilion unternehmen. Der Abschied schließlich lässt sich nicht nur durch Mitbringsel der örtlichen Weinproduktion versüßen, sondern auch durch Caudalies Hautpflegeserie auf Traubenbasis.

Buchtipp: »Der große Meaulnes« von Alain-Fournier

La vérité est dans le vin

On sait fort bien que le vin est excellent pour la santé. Ici, non seulement on le consomme, mais on peut également se baigner dedans.

Les Sources de Caudalie est un hôtel délicieux, dans tous les sens du terme. Il offre une remise en forme très particulière et ce au beau milieu d'un vignoble.

Pendant votre séance de vinothérapie, unique en son genre, vous aurez le choix entre un enveloppement Merlot, un massage Sauvignon ou une exfoliation Cabernet ; à moins que vous ne préfériez un traitement anti-âge et minceur fondé sur des dérivés du raisin, qui vous mettrait presque l'eau à la bouche.

Les gastronomes trouveront deux restaurants, ainsi qu'une cave de 15 000 bouteilles. Après le dîner, les fumeurs pourront se retirer dans la tour-bibliothèque, fief du club des amateurs de cigares. Les autres choieront leurs papilles gustatives en dégustant des grands crus dans le bar French Paradox.

Après avoir goûté aux plaisirs de la table et des soins de beauté, vous irez découvrir les châteaux viticoles environnants, à bicyclette ou en limousine, et les grands domaines des régions de Médoc, Sauternes, Pomerol et Saint-Émilion. En souvenir, vous emporterez quelques bouteilles de vin local et les fameux produits de beauté Caudalie.

Livres à emporter : « Le grand Meaulnes » d'Alain-Fournier « Les Cent plus beaux textes sur le vin » de Louis et Jean Orizet

ANREISE	15 Minuten südlich von Bordeaux
PREIS	Zimmer zwischen 175 und 240 €, Suiten zwischen 290 und 425 €, je nach Saison
ZIMMER	49 Zimmer und Suiten
KÜCHE	Ein wahres Fest für die Sinne
GESCHICHTE	Erbaut und eröffnet 1999
X-FAKTOR	Wein für Gaumen, Sinne und Körper

ACCÈS	À 15 minutes au sud de Bordeaux
PRIX	Chambres de 175 à 240 €, suites de 290 à 425 €, selon la saison
CHAMBRES	49 chambres et suites
RESTAURATION	Le nec plus ultra pour les sens
HISTOIRE	Construit et ouvert en 1999
LES « PLUS »	Du vin pour le goût, la santé, la beauté

Joie de vivre...
Les Prés d'Eugénie, Landes

Les Prés d'Eugénie, Landes

Joie de vivre

For some, this is a place of pilgrimage. Those who value fine dining come here to savour the great food and wine, devised by one of France's most well known chefs. This is Michel Guérard's resort, where the ambience is as delicious as the food. Les Prés d'Eugénie are a cluster of hotels, restaurants, and a health spa. They have been described as being the model for what a country retreat should be like. Indeed, this is the image of the good life. Guests are treated to a blend of herb gardens and climbing roses, exotic fragrances and delicious flavours, exquisite guestrooms, and sparkling springs. The mixing of such fine ingredients makes this a very inviting setting. The old adage that two cooks are better than one does not apply here. Michel reigns over the cuisine, and his wife Christine has created the rest. The buildings, gardens, and the spa are her realm, while the restaurant is a national treasure, in a country that is famous for its food.

The resort is in the village of Eugénie-les-Bains, in the heart of the Landes forest. It is a town so picturesque that it almost looks like a movie set.

Book to pack: "How Proust Can Change Your Life" by Alain de Botton

Les Prés d'Eugénie	
40320 Eugénie-les-Bains	
Landes	
France	
Tel : + 33 (0) 558 050 607	
Fax : + 33 (0)558 511 010	
E-mail: guerard@relaischateaux.fr	
Website: www.michelguerard.com	

DIRECTIONS	Les Prés d'Eugénie are located in the village of Eugénie-les-Bains, in the heart of the Aquitaine Region. Pau Airport is 45 km/28 m away, Bordeaux Airport is 120 km/74 m north
RATES	€ 182 to 365
ROOMS	35 rooms and apartments
FOOD	The raison d'être
HISTORY	Les Prés d'Eugénie were built in the 18th century and opened in 1862 as hotel
X-FACTOR	The art of living and eating

Joie de vivre

Wer gute Küche zu schätzen weiß, der kommt hierher, um hervorragendes Essen und große Weine zu genießen. Sie werden kredenzt von Michel Guérard, einem der bekanntesten Köche des Landes, der hier seinen Wirkungsort hat. Das Ambiente des Hotels steht jedoch dem Essen in seiner »Köstlichkeit« in nichts nach. Les Prés d'Eugénie ist ein Ensemble aus mehreren Hotels, Restaurants und einer Wellnessanlage. Auf ideale Weise wird einem hier ein ruhiges Leben auf dem Land, ein Sinnbild für das Leben, wie es sein sollte, geboten. Der Gast wird verwöhnt mit duftenden Kräutergärten und rankenden Rosen, exotischen Düften und köstlichen Aromen, exquisiten Gästezimmern und perlenden Quellen. Die perfekte Mischung dieser Zutaten macht den Ort so einladend. Dass viele Köche den Brei verderben, nun, das weiß Michel Guérard. Deshalb hat er die Oberhoheit über die Küche, und seine Frau Christine gestaltet den Rest der Anlage. Gebäude, Gärten und die Wellnessanlage sind ihr Reich, das Restaurant aber ist ein nationales Heiligtum. Die Hotelanlage liegt in dem malerischen Örtchen Eugénie-les-Bains, im Herzen der Wälder der Landes. Hier ist es so pittoresk, dass man sich in einer Spielfilmkulisse zu befinden glaubt.

Buchtipp: »Wie Proust Ihr Leben verändern kann« von Alain de Botton

Joie de vivre

Les amateurs de bonne chère viennent ici déguster d'excellents vins et une délicieuse cuisine concoctée par l'un des chefs les plus réputés de France. C'est le fief de Michel Guérard, et l'ambiance y est à la hauteur de la gastronomie. Les Prés d'Eugénie, qui regroupent plusieurs hôtels et restaurants ainsi qu'un centre thermal, ont été décrits comme un modèle de retraite champêtre. Pour beaucoup d'hôtes, il s'agit même d'un véritable lieu de pèlerinage. Il est vrai que le complexe est l'image même du « bien-être » : on y déambule parmi les plantes aromatiques et les roses grimpantes, les parfums exotiques et les odeurs alléchantes, les salons élégants et les sources d'eau chaude. Le mariage réussi de tous ces ingrédients forme un cadre résolument enchanteur. Michel Guérard règne sur la cuisine, dont l'éloge n'est plus à faire ; son épouse Christine s'occupe du reste : résidences, jardins et thermes.

Le complexe hôtelier se trouve à Eugénie-les-Bains, au cœur de la forêt landaise ; une petite ville si pittoresque qu'on la croirait créée pour un film.

Livre à emporter : « Comment Proust peut changer votre vie » d'Alain de Botton

ANREISE	Im Dorf Eugénie-les-Bains im Herzen von Aquitanien gelegen. Der Flughafen von Pau ist 45 km entfernt, der Flughafen von Bordeaux liegt 120 km nördlich von Eugénie-les-Bains	ACCÈS	Les Prés d'Eugénie sont situés à Eugénie-les-Bains, au centre de l'Aquitaine. L'aéroport de Pau se trouve à 45 km, celui de Bordeaux à 120 km au nord d'Eugénie-les-Bains
PREIS	Zwischen 182 und 365 €	PRIX	De 182 et 365 €
ZIMMER	35 Zimmer und Apartments	CHAMBRES	35 chambres et appartements
KÜCHE	La raison d'être	RESTAURATION	La raison d'être
GESCHICHTE	Die Gebäude stammen aus dem 18. Jahrhundert. Das Hotel wurde 1862 eröffnet	HISTOIRE	Construit au XVIIIe siècle, hôtel depuis 1862
X-FAKTOR	Die Kunst zu leben und die Kunst zu essen	LES « PLUS »	L'art de vivre dans toute sa splendeur

Far from the madding crowd.
Les Maisons Marines d'Huchet, Aquitaine

Les Maisons Marines d'Huchet, Aquitaine

Far from the madding crowd

A tall structure often marks the site of somewhere special. In a distant place in France, far from the crowds that flock to see his famous Parisian tower, there is a small marine beacon built by Gustave Eiffel. It also marks a special spot. On the Atlantic coast between Bordeaux and Biarritz there are many miles of deserted beaches, edged by forests of pine trees. Hidden amongst the sand dunes is a tiny retreat where the motto is "keep it simple". Les Maisons Marines consist of just three beach houses, an unusual trio. The distinctive main house was built some one hundred and fifty years ago as a hunting lodge. The other two houses, once boatsheds, are now charming little guest cottages set apart in this quiet hideaway.

Access to Les Maisons Marines is circuitous; there is no direct route to here, because first you must stay at one of Michel and Christine Guérard's hotels at Eugénie-les-Bains, like Les Prés d'Eugénie, to gain admittance to the beach houses. They are more like a private home than a hotel, one the owners invite you to share, and a special place to take time out and savour the solitude. The sound of the surf will lull you to sleep.

Book to pack: "Les Misérables" by Victor Hugo

Les Maisons Marines d'Huchet

40320 Eugénie-les-Bains
France
Tel: + 33 (0) 5 58 05 06 07
Fax: + 33 (0) 5 58 51 10 10
E-mail: guerard@relaischateaux.fr
Website: www.relaischateaux.fr/guerard

DIRECTIONS	150 km/93 m south from Bordeaux Airport
RATES	€ 183 to 366
ROOMS	2 houses that accommodate two people
FOOD	Menus by a master chef
HISTORY	Built in the middle of the 19th century, Les Maisons Marines opened as guesthouses in December 1999
X-FACTOR	Solitude and scenery with special surroundings and food

Abseits des Massentourismus

Es kommt häufig vor, dass ein Ort, der etwas Außergewöhnliches zu bieten hat, durch ein hohes Bauwerk gekennzeich-
net ist. In einem entlegenen Winkel an der Westküste
Frankreichs, weitab von den Touristenmassen, die sich um
seinen berühmten Turm in Paris drängen, steht ein kleines,
von Gustave Eiffel erbautes Leuchtfeuer, das mit Sicherheit
auf einen ganz besonderen Ort verweist.
Zwischen Bordeaux und Biarritz erstrecken sich entlang der
Atlantikküste lange, einsame Strände, die von Pinienwäldern
geschützt werden. Versteckt in den Sanddünen liegt ein
kleines Refugium, in dem das Motto »weniger ist mehr«
stilvoll gelebt wird. Les Maisons Marines sind genau drei
Strandhäuser: Das markante Haupthaus wurde vor etwa 150
Jahren als Jagdhütte erbaut. Die beiden anderen Gebäude
dienten früher als Bootshäuser und sind heute bezaubernde
kleine Ferienhäuschen, die ganz im Verborgenen liegen.
Es ist jedoch ein Umweg nötig, um nach Les Maisons
Marines zu kommen, denn Sie müssen zuvor in einem der
Hotels von Michel und Christine Guérard in Eugénie-les-
Bains, wie etwa dem Les Prés d'Eugénie, zu Gast gewesen
sein. In den Strandhäusern sind Sie dann eher privilegierter
Hausgast der Besitzer als Hotelbesucher. Nutzen Sie die
Abgeschiedenheit, um zur Ruhe zu kommen, und lassen Sie
sich nachts vom Rauschen des Meeres in den Schlaf wiegen.

Buchtipps: »Die Elenden« von Victor Hugo

Loin des foules

Il est fréquent qu'un lieu extraordinaire se distingue par un
bâtiment de haute taille. Dans un coin reculé de France, loin
des foules qui affluent pour visiter la célèbre tour Eiffel à
Paris, se trouve un petit phare également construit par
Gustave Eiffel, soulignant lui aussi un lieu remarquable.
De Bordeaux à Biarritz, la côte Atlantique s'étend sur des
kilomètres de plages désertes, bordées de forêts de pins.
Dans les dunes se cache une retraite minuscule où le mot
d'ordre est « simplicité ». Au nombre de trois, ces Maisons
Marines forment un trio original. La plus grande, d'aspect
distinctif, est un ancien pavillon de chasse construit il y a
environ 150 ans. Les deux autres, d'anciens hangars à bateaux,
sont aujourd'hui de charmantes petites maisons d'hôtes,
situées à l'écart dans cette retraite paisible.
L'accès aux Maisons Marines se fait par des chemins détour-
nés : pour y être admis, il faut d'abord séjourner dans l'un
des hôtels de Michel et Christine Guérard, à Eugénie-les-
Bains ou aux Prés d'Eugénie. Elles ressemblent moins à un
hôtel qu'à des demeures privées que leur propriétaire vous
aurait invité à partager. Dans ce lieu privilégié dont vous
savourerez la solitude, vous vous reposerez, bercé par le
clapotis des vagues.

Livre à emporter : « Les Misérables » de Victor Hugo

ANREISE	150 km südlich vom internationalen Flughafen Bordeaux
PREIS	Zwischen 183 und 366 €
ZIMMER	2 Häuser für je 2 Personen
KÜCHE	Menüs gekocht von einem Spitzenkoch
GESCHICHTE	Les Maisons Marines wurden Mitte des 19. Jahrhundert erbaut und werden seit Dezember 1999 als Gästehäuser genutzt
X-FAKTOR	Abgeschiedenheit, schöne Umgebung und hervorragen-des Essen

ACCÈS	À 150 km au sud de l'aéroport international de Bordeaux
PRIX	De 183 à 366 €
CHAMBRES	2 maisons accueillant deux personnes
RESTAURATION	Cuisine d'un chef cuisinier
HISTOIRE	Construites au milieu du XIXe siècle, Les Maisons Marines ouvraient leurs portes en décembre 1999
LES « PLUS »	Solitude, cadre superbe et gastronomie

Inner sanctum...
La Mirande, Avignon

La Mirande, Avignon

Inner sanctum

In medieval times, Avignon was the residence of several popes. Conflicts within the Catholic Church as well as between the Pope and the worldly powers are to be held responsible for this relocation.

The Pope's temporary displacement to Avignon resulted in a building fervour, as cardinals and prelates of the church strove to construct worthy earthly palaces and houses to dwell in. Originally the site of a 14th-century cardinal's residence, La Mirande is blessed with an ideal position. It is in the heart of the city, in a tranquil cobbled square, at the very foot of the Popes' Palace. Behind the hotel's original stone façade is an exquisite interior; one that bears testament to a real quest to attain a near faultless authenticity. Its success is such that even though it is relatively new, the interior seems to have evolved over generations and time. Meticulously restored, using the style and materials of the 17th and 18th century, La Mirande has all the splendour of an aristocratic residence of the era, together with the best of contemporary cuisine. Under the coffered ceiling of the restaurant, inventive fare that makes you truly grateful is served.

Books to pack: "All Men are Mortal" by Simone de Beauvoir "Tartarin de Tarascon" by Alphonse Daudet

La Mirande 4, Place de la Mirande 84000 Avignon France Tel: + 33 (0) 490 859 393 Fax: + 33 (0) 490 862 685 E-mail: mirande@la-mirande.fr Website: www.la-mirande.fr	

DIRECTIONS	2.5 hours south from Paris by TGV; in the centre of Avignon
RATES	€ 260 to 640
ROOMS	19 rooms and 1 suite
FOOD	Michelin-starred restaurant, Provencal and French cuisine, with a cooking school for disciples
HISTORY	Originally built in the 14th century, La Mirande was transformed several times over the centuries. The hotel was opened in 1990
X-FACTOR	Aristocratic interior and heavenly food

Im Allerheiligsten

Im Mittelalter war Avignon mehrfach für kurze Zeit Sitz des Papstes. Konflikte innerhalb der Kurie sowie zwischen Päpsten und weltlichen Mächten führten zu diesen unfreiwilligen Ortswechseln.

Begleitet wurde dieser kurzzeitige Umzug nach Avignon von einem wahren Bauboom, denn Kardinäle und Prälaten der Kirche machten es sich zur Aufgabe, schon auf Erden Paläste und Häuser zu errichten, die ihrer würdig waren. Wo heute das Hotel La Mirande steht, befand sich im 14. Jahrhundert die Residenz eines Kardinals. Auch strategisch liegt das Hotel himmlisch, mitten im Herzen der Stadt nämlich, an einem verträumten Platz mit Kopfsteinpflaster, direkt am Fuß des Papstpalastes. Hinter der Originalfassade des Hotels versteckt sich ein herrliches Interieur, das auf Schritt und Tritt das Bestreben erkennen lässt, so viel Authentizität wie möglich herzustellen. Obwohl noch gar nicht alt, wirkt die Innengestaltung, als hätten an ihr ganze Generationen und Zeitläufte gewirkt.

Im Stil des 17. und 18. Jahrhunderts bis ins Detail restauriert, strahlt La Mirande die Pracht einer aristokratischen Residenz aus und bietet gleichzeitig das Beste aus der heutigen Küche. Unter der Kassettendecke des Restaurants wird kreative Kochkunst geboten, die zu wahren Dankesgebeten verleitet.

Buchtipps: »Alle Menschen sind sterblich« von Simone de Beauvoir

»Die Abenteuer des Herrn Tartarin aus Tarascon« von Alphonse Daudet

Inner sanctum

Au Moyen Âge, Avignon devint pendant plusieurs courtes périodes la ville des Papes, lorsque des conflits au sein de la curie et entre la papauté et les pouvoirs temporels conduisirent à ce changement de résidence involontaire.

L'installation du Pape en Avignon entraîna un boom dans la construction, les cardinaux et prélats rivalisant dans l'édification de palais et demeures luxueuses. Autrefois résidence d'un cardinal du XIVe siècle, l'hôtel La Mirande jouit d'une situation privilégiée. En plein cœur de la ville, sur une paisible place pavée, il se dresse au pied du Palais des Papes. Derrière la façade d'origine, se cache un ravissant intérieur qui se targue de rechercher une authenticité quasi parfaite. Cela avec grand succès, car bien qu'il soit relativement récent, l'intérieur de La Mirande semble avoir évolué au fil des générations et du temps.

Méticuleusement restauré, dans le style et les matériaux des XVIIe et XVIIIe siècles, l'hôtel possède toute la splendeur d'une résidence aristocratique d'époque. S'y ajoute une cuisine contemporaine de grand chef ; sous le plafond à caissons du restaurant, de superbes plats originaux vous seront servis.

Livres à emporter : «Tous les hommes sont mortels» de Simone de Beauvoir

«Aventures prodigieuses de Tartarin de Tarascon» d'Alphonse Daudet

ANREISE	2,5 Stunden Fahrt südlich von Paris mit dem TGV. Im Zentrum von Avignon gelegen
PREIS	Zwischen 260 und 640 €
ZIMMER	19 Zimmer und 1 Suite
KÜCHE	Vom Guide Michelin ausgezeichnetes Restaurant mit provenzalischer und französischer Küche. Eine Kochschule ist dem Restaurant angeschlossen
GESCHICHTE	Erbaut im 14. Jahrhundert, mehrfach über die Jahrhunderte umgebaut und 1990 als Hotel eröffnet
X-FAKTOR	Aristokratisches Interieur und himmlisches Essen

ACCÈS	À 2 heures 30 au sud de Paris en TGV ; en plein centre-ville d'Avignon
PRIX	De 260 à 640 €
CHAMBRES	19 chambres et 1 suite
RESTAURATION	2 étoiles au Michelin, cuisine française et provençale. Cours de cuisine pour les adeptes
HISTOIRE	Construit au XIVe siècle, le bâtiment a été transformé plusieurs fois au cours des siècles. L'hôtel a ouvert en 1990
LES « PLUS »	Intérieur aristocratique et cuisine succulente

A providential place...
La Bastide de Marie, Ménerbes

La Bastide de Marie, Ménerbes

A providential place

To have a centuries-old house with its own vineyard in one of the most beautiful parts of France, in reach of charming villages, has been a dream of many.

High in the Lubéron Mountains of Provence, that fantasy can come partly true by staying at La Bastide de Marie, a small inn more like a home than a hotel. Set in a vineyard that produces promising red, white, and rosé Côtes du Lubéron, the rustic old farmhouse has been given a new lease of life. Contemporary restful colours, and the peace and quiet of the setting make this a haven for travellers who crave tranquillity and nourishment of body and mind. When the air is scented with lavender, sunlight bathes the walled garden, and delectable food and wine is served beside the pool, one could dream of not going home.

On a nearby hillside is the picturesque village of Ménerbes. This may be as far as guests of La Bastide de Marie might want to venture. For those who feel like going further on shopping expeditions, there are lively weekly markets in the surrounding countryside, specialising in collectables from pottery to antiques.

Books to pack: "The Water of the Hills" by Marcel Pagnol "Perfume" by Patrick Süskind

La Bastide de Marie
Route de Bonnieux
Quartier de la Verrerie
84560 Ménerbes
France
Tel: + 33 (0)4 90 72 30 20
Fax: + 33 (0)4 90 72 54 20
E-mail: bastidemarie@c-h-m.com
Website: www.c-h-m.com

DIRECTIONS	An hour's drive north from Marseille Airport, 40 minutes east from the airport of Avignon; 2.5 hours with TGV south from Paris
RATES	Rooms from € 370 to 450, suites from € 565 to 640 inclusive of all but lunch or dinner
ROOMS	8 rooms and 4 suites
FOOD	The best of Provencal cuisine
HISTORY	Built in the 18th century, La Bastide de Marie was opened as a hotel in 2000
X-FACTOR	A taste of Provence the way it should be

Ein schicksalhafter Ort

Wer hat nicht schon einmal davon geträumt, Besitzer eines
jahrhundertealten Hauses mit eigenem Weinberg zu sein,
welches in einer der schönsten Regionen Frankreichs liegt,
umgeben von charmanten Dörfern?
Zumindest für eine Weile können Sie sich diesen Traum
hoch in den Lubéron-Bergen der Provence in La Bastide de
Marie erfüllen, einem bezaubernden, kleinen Hotel, das fast
wie ein Zuhause ist. Inmitten eines Weinbergs gelegen, der
viel versprechenden roten, weißen und rosé Côtes du Lubéron
hervorbringt, erlebt dieses rustikale alte Bauernhaus einen
zweiten Frühling. Angenehme, ruhige Farben und die friedliche Umgebung machen es zu einer Zuflucht für Reisende,
die sich nach stressfreier Erholung für Körper und Seele
sehnen. Wenn Lavendelduft in der Luft liegt, die Sonne auf
dem von Mauern geschützten Garten liegt und köstliche
Gerichte und Weine am Pool serviert werden, lässt es sich
leicht davon träumen, für immer zu bleiben.
Auf einem nahe gelegenen Hügel liegt das malerische
Dörfchen Ménerbes. Und weiter möchten sich viele Gäste
von La Bastide de Marie möglicherweise gar nicht entfernen.
Wer aber gern auch mal einen Einkaufsbummel unternimmt,
sollte die lebhaften Wochenmärkte in den Dörfern der Umgebung besuchen, wo Sammlerstücke von Töpferwaren bis
zu Antiquitäten angeboten werden.
**Buchtipps: »Die Wasser der Hügel« von Marcel Pagnol
»Das Parfum« von Patrick Süskind**

Un lieu providentiel

Nombreux sont ceux qui rêvent de posséder une vieille
maison nichée au cœur des vignes, non loin de charmants
villages, dans l'une de ces belles régions de France.
Ce rêve se réalise le temps d'un séjour à La Bastide de
Marie, une petite auberge perchée dans les Montagnes du
Lubéron, qui évoque davantage une maison de famille qu'un
hôtel. Située dans un vignoble produisant d'excellents Côtes
du Lubéron rouges, blancs et rosés, cette ancienne ferme
a trouvé une nouvelle jeunesse. Le décor aux couleurs
reposantes et le cadre serein en font un havre de paix pour
qui a soif de quiétude et recherche à la fois des nourritures
spirituelles et terrestres. Séduit par l'air embaumant la
lavande, par le soleil qui baigne le jardin clos et par les mets
et vins délicieux servis près de la piscine, on s'imaginerait
bien de ne plus jamais rentrer chez soi.
Sur une colline voisine s'élève le pittoresque village de
Ménerbes. Parfois, les hôtes de La Bastide de Marie ne souhaitent pas s'aventurer plus loin. Les marchés hebdomadaires
des environs offrent toutes sortes d'objets, des faïences aux
antiquités.
**Livre à emporter : « Manon des sources » de Marcel Pagnol
« Le Parfum » de Patrick Süskind**

ANREISE	1 Fahrstunde nördlich vom Flughafen Marseille, 40 Minuten nach Osten vom Flughafen Avignon; 2,5 Stunden Fahrt südlich von Paris mit dem TGV
PREIS	Zimmer zwischen 370 und 450 €, Suiten zwischen 565 und 640 € einschließlich Frühstück und Abendessen
ZIMMER	8 Zimmer und 4 Suiten
KÜCHE	Das Beste aus der provenzalischen Küche
GESCHICHTE	Im 18. Jahrhundert erbaut, 2000 als Hotel eröffnet
X-FAKTOR	Die Provence von ihrer Glanzseite

ACCÈS	À une heure de route au nord de l'aéroport de Marseille, à 40 minutes à l'est de l'aéroport d'Avignon. À 2 heures 30 au sud de Paris en TGV
PRIX	Chambres de 370 à 450 €, suites de 565 à 640 €, petit déjeuner et dîner compris
CHAMBRES	8 chambres et 4 suites
RESTAURATION	Le meilleur de la cuisine provençale
HISTOIRE	Construite au XVIIIe, La Bastide de Marie est un hôtel depuis 2000
LES « PLUS »	La Provence authentique

A place in the country...
La Maison Domaine de Bournissac, Provence

La Maison Domaine de Bournissac, Provence

A place in the country

Just minutes from the town of Saint-Rémy, in the heart of Provence, there is an old country inn. It is still quite a secret place, even in this much-explored area.

Hidden at the end of a long gravel road, a simple house comes into view. Yet the Domaine de Bournissac has a deceptive exterior; the inside is not quite as simple as it appears to be. The centuries-old farmhouse has been restored; revived as an oasis of calm. Style and simplicity have been expertly paired. The pale colours of marble, stone, and bleached wood signal the restful atmosphere to be found within its walls. Each room is different; but all are in soft colours and composed by a sure and artistic hand. Outside, the garden and terrace are places to sit in the sun and dream. A massive old oak tree casts a welcome shade. In the summer, fields of sunflowers and lavender are in bloom. This is the landscape and light that so inspired Van Gogh, and lures people to it still.

However, despite its past, traditional farmhouse style food is not on the menu. The kitchen has a reputation that has spread a long way from its rural setting.

Book to pack: "Lust for Life: the Story of Vincent van Gogh" by Irving Stone

La Maison Domaine de Bournissac

Montée d'Eyragues

13550 Paluds de Noves

France

Tel: + 33 (0) 490902525

Fax: + 33 (0) 490902526

E-mail: annie@lamaison-a-bournissac.com

Website: www.lamaison-a-bournissac.com

DIRECTIONS	South of Avignon, it is just 5 minutes from Saint-Rémy-de-Provence
RATES	From € 89 to 206
ROOMS	13 rooms
FOOD	Renowned, and drawing on the rich local resources
HISTORY	Part of the building dates back to the 14th century, others are from the 18th century. The Domaine de Bournissac has received guests since 1999
X-FACTOR	A lovely country house in one of the most beautiful parts of France

Ein Platz auf dem Lande

Nur wenige Minuten von Saint-Rémy im Herzen der Provence liegt ein alter Landgasthof. Er ist sogar in dieser touristisch weitgehend erschlossenen Gegend ein Geheimtipp geblieben.

Versteckt am Ende eines langen Kieswegs entdeckt man plötzlich ein einfaches Haus. Doch dieser Eindruck täuscht: Die Domaine de Bournissac wirkt nur äußerlich einfach. Das ehemalige, mehrere Jahrhunderte alte Bauernhaus ist heute als Oase der Stille wieder zum Leben erwacht. Stil und Schlichtheit sind eine perfekte Symbiose eingegangen. Die blasse Farbpalette von Marmor, Stein und gebleichtem Holz signalisiert, welch entspannende Atmosphäre innerhalb der Steinmauern zu finden ist. Die Gästezimmer wurden jeweils indiviuell gestaltet, alle jedoch gekonnt und stilsicher und in warmen Farben gehalten. Draußen laden Garten und Terrasse zum Sonnenbaden und Träumen ein, und eine riesige alte Eiche spendet angenehmen Schatten. Im Sommer blühen Sonnenblumen und Lavendel in den Feldern ringsherum. Landschaft und Licht inspirierten einst Van Gogh und ziehen bis heute die Menschen an.

Doch etwas überrascht: Trotz der langen Geschichte des Hofs wird hier keine deftige Landhausküche serviert, sondern Gerichte, die die ländlichen Wurzeln längst hinter sich gelassen haben.

Buchtipp: »Vincent van Gogh. Ein Leben in Leidenschaft« von Irving Stone

Dans la campagne provençale

À quelques minutes à peine de Saint-Rémy, en plein cœur de la Provence, se dresse une vieille auberge de campagne. C'est un endroit encore secret dans cette région qui n'en compte plus guère.

Tout au bout d'une longue route de gravier surgit une maison toute simple. Mais que l'on ne s'y trompe pas : l'intérieur est beaucoup moins modeste qu'il n'y paraît. Cette ancienne ferme séculaire a été restaurée, transformée en une oasis de tranquillité, où raffinement et simplicité vont de pair. Les teintes discrètes du marbre, de la pierre et du bois brut annoncent l'atmosphère paisible qui règne entre ses murs. Chaque chambre est différente des autres, mais toutes sont dotées de couleurs douces et décorées avec beaucoup de goût. À l'extérieur, le jardin et la terrasse se prêtent au repos et à la rêverie, à l'ombre d'un imposant chêne centenaire. En été, les champs de tournesol et de lavande déploient leurs symphonies de couleurs. C'est le paysage et la lumière qui ont inspiré Van Gogh, et qui continuent d'attirer les visiteurs.

En dépit de son passé rural, l'auberge ne sert pas de plats campagnards : l'excellente cuisine a depuis longtemps oublié ses origines champêtres.

Livre à emporter : « La Vie passionnée de Vincent van Gogh » de Irving Stone

ANREISE	Südlich von Avignon und 5 Minuten von Saint-Rémy-de-Provence entfernt
PREIS	Zwischen 89 und 206 €
ZIMMER	13 Zimmer
KÜCHE	Renommierte Küche, die sich am kulinarischen Reichtum der Region orientiert
GESCHICHTE	Teile des Gebäudes stammen aus dem 14. Jahrhundert, andere aus dem 18. Jahrhundert. Die Domaine de Bournissac ist seit 1999 Hotel
X-FAKTOR	Ein wunderschönes Landhaus in einem wunderschönen Teil Frankreichs

ACCÈS	Au sud d'Avignon, à 5 minutes de Saint-Rémy-de-Provence
PRIX	De 89 à 206 €
CHAMBRES	13 chambres
RESTAURATION	Réputée, tire profit des ressources locales
HISTOIRE	Quelques parties du bâtiment sont du XIVe siècle, les autres du XVIIIe siècle ; le Domaine de Bournissac est un hôtel depuis 1999
LES « PLUS »	Une ravissante maison de campagne dans une région non moins superbe

A poetic hideaway...
Villa Fiordaliso, Lago di Garda

Villa Fiordaliso, Lago di Garda

A poetic hideaway

There is a romantic air of time gone by here. The view is much the same across the lake as it was when the poet Gabriele D'Annunzio looked out from his window. Perhaps he had writer's block and was hoping to be inspired as he gazed at the tranquil waters.

Villa Fiordaliso is an ideal place to hide away, whether or not you are prone to poetry or prose. The setting is poetic in itself. Framed by cypresses, pine, and olive trees; and on the edge of Lake Garda, the elegant old villa has a sense of absolute calm. No doubt, if the walls of the classic interior could speak, many anecdotes might be told of those who have stayed here, from poets to dictators. For utter romantics, there is a most enticing place close by; the city of Verona, famed for being the source of the tragic love story of Romeo and Juliet. Walking through the streets and underneath the balconies of the "pair of star-crossed lovers", you believe the tale to be true.

You will very likely become lyrical over the cuisine, since the menu may not have been written by a poet, but is certainly cooked by artists. Parting from Villa Fiordaliso will indeed be an occasion for "sweet sorrow".

**Books to pack: "Romeo and Juliet" by William Shakespeare
"The Flame" by Gabriele D'Annunzio**

Villa Fiordaliso
Via Zanardelli 150
25083 Gardone Riviera
Italy
Tel: + 39 (0) 365 201 58
Fax: + 39 (0) 365 290 011
E-mail: fiordaliso@relaischateaux.com
Website: www.relaischateaux.com

DIRECTIONS	40 km/25 m north-west of Verona
RATES	€ 181 to 491
ROOMS	7 rooms
FOOD	A Michelin-starred restaurant
X-FACTOR	Utterly romantic

Ein malerisches Versteck

An diesem Ort spürt man den Zauber vergangener Zeiten.
Der Blick über den See ist noch derselbe wie damals, als der
Dichter Gabriele D'Annunzio aus seinem Fenster schaute.
Vielleicht hatte er einen Schreibblock dabei und ließ sich
von dem ruhigen Gewässer vor seinen Augen inspirieren.
Die Villa Fiordaliso ist ein idealer Ort, um sich zurückzu-
ziehen. Allein die Landschaft ist reinste Poesie! In der von
Zypressen, Pinien und Olivenbäumen eingerahmten alten
Villa am Ufer des Gardasees herrscht absolute Stille. Wenn
die Wände des klassischen Interieurs reden könnten, wür-
den sie zweifellos hübsche kleine Anekdoten über die vielen
berühmten Persönlichkeiten – ob Dichter oder Diktatoren –
erzählen, die hier genächtigt haben. Romantiker finden ganz
in der Nähe einen besonders reizvollen Ort, nämlich die Stadt
Verona, die durch die tragische Liebesgeschichte von Romeo
und Julia weltberühmt wurde. Wenn man durch die Straßen
und unter den Balkonen entlangpromeniert, könnte man fast
glauben, die Geschichte habe sich wirklich zugetragen.
Die Küche der Villa Fiordaliso ist ein wahres Gedicht, und
auch wenn die Speisekarte vielleicht nicht von Dichterhand
geschrieben wurde, sind es doch Künstler, die hier wirken.
Buchtipps: »Romeo und Julia« von William Shakespeare
»Das Feuer« von Gabriele D'Annunzio

Un refuge romantique

Il flotte ici un air de nostalgie romantique. La vue sur le lac
est sûrement très semblable à celle dont jouissait le poète
Gabriele D'Annunzio depuis sa fenêtre. Devant une page
blanche, peut-être recherchait-il l'inspiration en contemplant
ces eaux paisibles…
La Villa Fiordaliso est un refuge idéal, même pour ceux qui
ne taquinent pas la plume. Le cadre est un poème à lui seul :
cernée de cyprès, de pins et d'oliviers, solitaire sur une rive
du lac de Garde, l'élégante villa ancienne respire le calme
absolu. Si les murs de l'édifice néoclassique pouvaient parler,
ils ne tariraient pas d'anecdotes sur ses résidents – des poètes
aux dictateurs. Pour les esprits romantiques, la ville de
Vérone, théâtre des tragiques amours de Roméo et Juliette,
se trouve à proximité. Une promenade dans les ruelles et
sous les balcons vous fera peut-être croire à l'histoire des
malheureux amants.
Mais réservez plutôt votre lyrisme pour la table : si la carte
n'a pas été rédigée par un poète, les mets sont certainement
cuisinés par de véritables artistes.
Livres à emporter : « Le Feu » de Gabriele D'Annunzio
« Roméo et Juliette » de William Shakespeare

ANREISE	40 km nordwestlich von Verona		ACCÈS	À 40 km au nord-est de Vérone
PREIS	Zwischen 181 und 491 €		PRIX	De 181 à 491 €
ZIMMER	7 Zimmer		CHAMBRES	7 chambres
KÜCHE	Ein mit mehreren Michelin-Sternen ausgezeichnetes Restaurant		RESTAURATION	Plusieurs étoiles au Michelin
X-FAKTOR	Romantik pur		LES « PLUS »	Le summum du romantisme

A world afloat...
Hotel Cipriani & Palazzo Vendramin, Venezia

Hotel Cipriani & Palazzo Vendramin, Venezia

A world afloat

"Streets flooded. Please advise." So said a telegram once sent from here by a humorous writer. But seriously, there is not much that can match the first sight of Venice. You should choose to arrive by boat; the ride along the Grand Canal, past palaces and churches, then turning into the lagoon of San Marco to see the sunlight glinting on the domes of the Doge's Palace, is a memorable one. The boat will bring you to Palazzo Vendramin. The 15th-century residence is on one of the many islands that make up this ancient city. The Palazzo's beautiful arched windows frame one of the most romantic and famous views in the world: the front-row view of St. Mark's Square. With only a few suites, it is more akin to an elegant private home; but it is part of the famed Hotel Cipriani, which is a short stroll away across a courtyard. Guests may share in all of that hotel's wealth of resources. Just a few minutes from its calm cloisters is a busier, noisier place. This special city of the past is quite like a magnet. Yet, off the main sightseer trail, there is a quieter, slower Venice still to be glimpsed.

Books to pack: "Death In Venice" by Thomas Mann
"A Venetian Reckoning" by Donna Leon

Hotel Cipriani & Palazzo Vendramin	
Isola della Giudecca, 10	
30133 Venezia	
Italy	
Tel: +39 (0) 41 5207744	
Fax: +39 (0) 41 5207745	
E-mail: info@hotelcipriani.it	
Website: www.hotelcipriani.it	

DIRECTIONS	30 minutes by boat from Marco Polo Airport
RATES	From € 1,558 to 3,723, including breakfast
ROOMS	15 suites and junior suites in the Palazzo Vendramin and the Palazzetto Nani Barbaro
FOOD	The cuisine of the Cipriani and the Cip's Club is worth being marooned on an island for
HISTORY	The Palazzo Vendramin was built in the 15th century and opened as a hotel in 1991, the Palazzetto Nani Barbaro opened in 1998
X-FACTOR	One of the ultimate locations.

Eine Welt im Fluss

»Alle Straßen unter Wasser. Was ist zu tun?«, lautete das Telegramm, das ein Schriftsteller mit Humor hier einst aufgab. Doch im Ernst: Der erste Anblick von Venedig lässt sich mit nichts vergleichen.

Wenn es geht, sollte man in der Stadt mit dem Boot ankommen. Die Fahrt auf dem Canal Grande vorbei an Palazzi und Kirchen, der Blick in die Lagune von San Marco, wenn die Sonne über den Dogenpalast dahingleitet, ist unvergesslich. Mit dem Boot gelangen Sie auch zum Palazzo Vendramin, einem Anwesen aus dem 15. Jahrhundert, das auf einer der vielen Inseln Venedigs liegt. Von hier aus bietet sich – gerahmt durch die Bogenfenster des Palazzo – ein fantastischer Blick auf den Markusplatz – einer der schönsten, berühmtesten und romantischsten Ausblicke der Welt. Der Palazzo erinnert mit seinen wenigen Suiten eher an ein elegantes Privathaus als an ein Hotel. Doch ist er Teil des berühmten Hotel Cipriani, das sich in einem wenige Minuten dauernden Spaziergang quer über einen Innenhof erreichen lässt. Den Gästen des Palazzo stehen die vielfältigen Angebote des Cipriani ebenfalls zur Verfügung. Nur wenige Minuten von der fast klösterlichen Ruhe und Beschaulichkeit entfernt, können sie in ein bunteres und lauteres Leben eintauchen.

Venedig scheint eine Stadt aus der Vergangenheit zu sein, doch ihre Anziehungskraft ist bis heute ungebrochen. Wie schön, dass es neben den typischen Touristenattraktionen noch ein leiseres und ruhigeres Venedig zu entdecken gibt.

Buchtipps: »Der Tod in Venedig« von Thomas Mann
»Venezianische Scharade« von Donna Leon

Entre terre et eau

« Rues inondées. Que faire ? ». Tel est le message télégraphique qu'envoya un visiteur de Venise qui ne manquait pas d'humour! Trêve de plaisanteries; rien ou presque n'égale l'impact de la première vision de Venise.

Arrivez de préférence à Venise par bateau. Le trajet le long du Grand Canal et de ses palais et églises, puis l'entrée dans la lagune de Saint-Marc pour voir le soleil scintiller sur les toits du Palais des Doges, est tout à fait mémorable. Le bateau vous amènera au Palazzo Vendramin. Cette résidence du XVe siècle se dresse sur l'une des nombreuses îles qui forment la ville ancienne. Le Palazzo donne sur la place Saint-Marc; ses superbes fenêtres en plein cintre encadrent l'une des places les plus romantiques et célèbres du monde. N'abritant que quelques suites, il évoque une élégante résidence privée, bien qu'il fasse partie de l'illustre hôtel Cipriani, situé seulement à quelques pas, de l'autre côté de la cour. Ses hôtes peuvent profiter de tout ce que le Cipriani a à offrir. À quelques minutes à peine de la tranquillité de ses murs, s'étend une place bruyante et fort animée.

Cette ville d'un autre temps est en effet un véritable aimant touristique. Néanmoins, au-delà des sentiers battus, se cache une Venise plus nonchalante et sereine .

Livres à emporter : « La Mort à Venise » de Thomas Mann
« Un Vénitien anonyme » de Donna Leon

ANREISE	30 Minuten Anfahrt mit dem Boot vom Marco Polo Flughafen
PREIS	Zwischen 1558 und 3723 €, Frühstück inklusive
ZIMMER	15 Suiten und Juniorsuiten im Palazzo Vendramin und dem Palazzetto Nani Barbaro
KÜCHE	Für die Küche des Cipriani und des Cip's Club kann man schon freiwillig zum Schiffbrüchigen werden ...
GESCHICHTE	Der Palazzo Vendramin wurde im 15. Jahrhundert erbaut. Er öffnete als Hotel im Jahr 1991, der Palazzetto Nani Barbaro 1998
X-FAKTOR	Einer der unvergleichlichsten Orte der Welt

ACCÈS	À 30 minutes de bateau de l'aéroport Marco Polo
PRIX	De 1558 à 3723 €, petit déjeuner compris
CHAMBRES	Le Palazzo Vendramin et le Palazzetto Nani Barbaro comptent 15 suites et junior suites
RESTAURATION	Se retrouver sur une île loin de tout, mais avec la table du Cipriani et du Cip's Club ...
HISTOIRE	Le Palazzo Vendramin a été construit au XVe siècle. Il ouvrait ses portes en 1991, le Palazzetto Nani Barbaro en 1998
LES « PLUS »	Un nec plus ultra à Venise

In a blue mood...

Grand Hotel Parco dei Principi, Sorrento

Grand Hotel Parco dei Principi, Sorrento

In a blue mood

According to the legend, the mermaids who tempted Ulysses with their enchanting songs lived in the Sorrentine Sea.
In the real world, the charms of the Grand Hotel Parco dei Principi has lured other travellers to that same coastline. Built on a cliff in one of the most famous gardens in Italy, the hotel's clean lines and cool blue and white decor seem to reflect the colour of the sea below. Master architect Gio Ponti created the hotel in the 1960s, applying his one-colour theory of interior design to striking effect, from the tiled floors to the window blinds.

The spacious terraces offer a dazzling view of the blue Bay of Naples and the volcano of Mount Vesuvius. An elevator or stairway built into an ancient cave takes the guests down to the hotel's private jetty and beach. Or bathers may prefer the swimming pool, secluded in the historic park that was once the property of various noble families.

Nearby is the picturesque town of Sorrento that crowns the rocky cliffs close to the end of the peninsula. In the cafés you can taste delicious cakes, ice cream, and a glass of "Limoncello", the local lemon liqueur, just some of the many attractions of this much-celebrated place.

Books to pack: "The Island of the Day Before" by Umberto Eco "Thus Spoke Bellavista: Naples, Love and Liberty" by Luciano De Crescenzo

Grand Hotel Parco dei Principi		
Via Rota 1	DIRECTIONS	On the outskirts of Sorrento, 48 km/30 m south from Naples
80067 Sorrento	RATES	€ 180 to 350
Italy	ROOMS	173 rooms, open from April to October; ask for a room with sea view
Tel: + 39 (0) 81 878 46 44		
Fax: + 39 (0) 81 878 37 86	FOOD	Neapolitan cuisine and local specialties in a beautiful restaurant
E-mail: info@grandhotelparcodeiprincipi.it	HISTORY	Built and opened in 1962
Website: www.grandhotelparcodeiprincipi.it	X-FACTOR	Enduring style in a stunning location

Blaue Stunde

Der Legende zufolge war es vor Sorrent, wo Odysseus und seine Gefährten von den Gesängen der Sirenen betört wurden. In der realen Welt werden indes andere Reisende vom Zauber des Grand Hotels Parco dei Principi an diese Küste gelockt. Die klaren Linien und das kühle Blau und Weiß dieses auf einer Steilküste aus Tuffstein erbauten Hotels, welches inmitten eines der berühmtesten Gärten Italiens liegt, scheinen das Farbenspiel des Meeres widerzuspiegeln. Der Meisterarchitekt Gio Ponti, der das Hotel in den 1960er-Jahren entwarf, hat hier seine Philosophie von einer monochromen Innenraumgestaltung mit spektakulärem Erfolg umgesetzt: von den gekachelten Fußböden bis hin zu den Jalousien.

Die großzügigen Terrassen bieten fantastische Ausblicke auf die blaue Bucht von Neapel und den Vesuv. Über einen Aufzug oder eine Treppe, die durch das Innere des Tuffsteins führt, gelangen Gäste zu dem Privatstrand des Hotels, der auch über einen eigenen Steg verfügt. Wassernixen können sich natürlich auch im Pool tummeln. Dieser liegt versteckt in dem historischen Park, der sich früher im Besitz verschiedener Adelsfamilien befand.

In der Nähe liegt die malerische Stadt Sorrent auf den Felsklippen am Ende der Halbinsel. Hier können Sie sich in den Cafés an köstlichem Kuchen, Eis-Spezialitäten und einem Glas Limoncello, dem in der Region produzierten Zitronenlikör, erbauen, um dann eine der zahlreichen Sehenswürdigkeiten dieses viel gepriesenen Ortes zu erkunden.

Buchtipps: »Die Insel des vorigen Tages« von Umberto Eco »Also sprach Bellavista. Neapel, Liebe und Freiheit« von Luciano De Crescenzo

Conte bleu

Selon la légende, les sirènes qui séduisirent Ulysse et ses compagnons par leur chant trompeur vivaient dans la mer de Sorrente.

Dans le monde réel, les charmes du Grand Hôtel Parco dei Principi ont attiré d'autres voyageurs vers ce littoral. Les lignes pures et le décor bleu et blanc de l'hôtel, construit sur une falaise dans l'un des jardins les plus célèbres d'Italie, semblent refléter les couleurs de la mer qui danse à ses pieds. Du carrelage aux stores, le célèbre architecte Gio Ponti, qui a créé l'hôtel dans les années 1960, a appliqué avec bonheur sa théorie selon laquelle la décoration d'intérieur se doit d'être monochrome.

Depuis les terrasses spacieuses, on découvre une vue éblouissante sur la mer bleue de la baie de Naples et sur le Vésuve. Les clients de l'hôtel descendent à la jetée et à la plage privées par un ascenseur ou un escalier qui traverse une grotte ancienne. On peut aussi se baigner dans la piscine, cachée dans le parc historique qui a appartenu autrefois à diverses familles nobles.

Tout près, la ville pittoresque de Sorrente couronne les falaises rocheuses proches de l'extrémité de la péninsule. Dans les salons de thé, on peut goûter aux gâteaux délicieux, aux glaces ou au limoncello, la liqueur de citron locale, quelques-uns seulement des nombreux attraits de cet endroit si célèbre.

Livres à emporter: « L'Ile du jour d'avant » d'Umberto Eco « Ainsi parlait Bellavista » de Luciano De Crescenzo

ANREISE	Am Stadtrand von Sorrent, 48 km südlich von Neapel
PREIS	Zwischen 180 und 350 €
ZIMMER	173 Zimmer, Öffnungszeiten April bis Oktober; fragen Sie nach einem Zimmer mit Meerblick
KÜCHE	Neapolitanische Küche und lokale Spezialitäten in einem wunderschönen, eleganten Restaurant
GESCHICHTE	Erbaut und geöffnet 1962
X-FAKTOR	Zeitloser Stil in atemberaubender Umgebung

ACCÈS	Dans les environs de Sorrente, à 48 km au sud de Naple
PRIX	De 180 à 350 €
CHAMBRES	173 chambres ; demandez une chambre avec vue sur la mer. Ouvert d'avril à octobre
RESTAURATION	Cuisine napolitaine et spécialités locales servies dans un restaurant splendide
HISTOIRE	Construit et ouvert en 1962
LES « PLUS »	Style intemporel, dans un cadre éblouissant

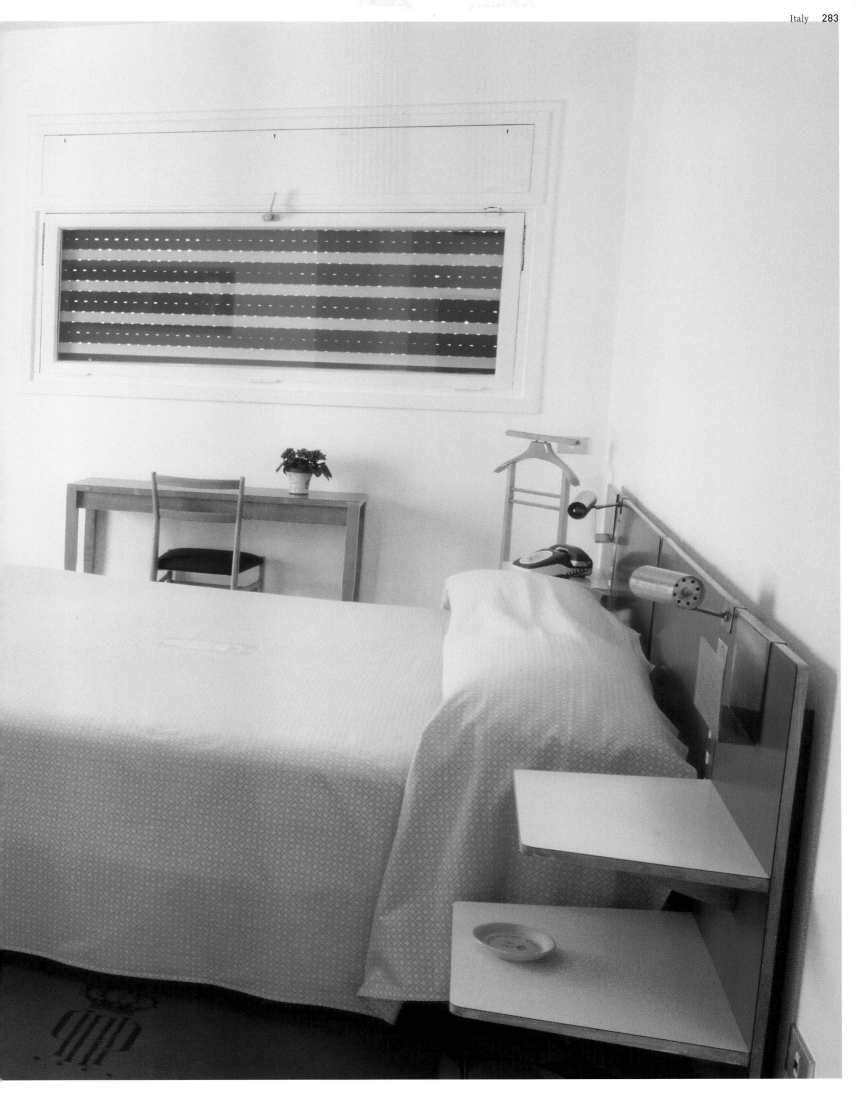

Changing rooms...
L'Atelier sul Mare, Sicilia

L' Atelier sul Mare, Sicilia

Changing rooms

Without doubt, guests here will ask to stay in a room other than the one in which they spent the last night.

At L'Atelier sul Mare, it is usual to change rooms daily so the guest can profit from being at this unique hotel as much as possible. Just a few steps from the sea in one of Sicily's most beautiful bays, on the coast between Palermo and Messina, the hotel has a rare concept: a place where the rooms double up as exhibition pieces. Well-known artists have created many of the rooms. The interiors that have sprung from their fertile imaginations are quite fantastic and dramatic spaces, all with poetic names. Dreams amongst the Drawings is themed around the growth of writing, The Prophet's Room pays homage to film director Pasolini, and in The Tower of Sigismondo, a circular tower descends from the transparent ceiling. At the base, an enormous round bed rotates slowly.

This might seem more like a museum than a hotel, except for the fact that, as its creator explains, "only when a visitor enters and lives in a room will the work of art be fully realized; the use of the room is an integral and fundamental part of the work."

Books to pack: "The Leopard" by Giuseppe Tomasi di Lampedusa "The Lives of the Artists" by Giorgio Vasari

L'Atelier sul Mare		
4, Via Cesare Battisti		
98079 Castel di Tusa (Messina)		
Sicily		
Italy		
Tel: + 39 (0) 921 334295		
Fax: + 39 (0) 921 334283		
E-mail: ateliersulmare@nebro.net		
Website: www.mediterraneo.it		
	DIRECTIONS	2 hours' drive west from Palermo, near the town of Cefalù
	RATES	Standard rooms from € 54, for the Art Rooms from € 80 to 90, breakfast included
	ROOMS	40 rooms and suites; 24 standard rooms decorated by young European artists, 14 rooms created by contemporary artists
	FOOD	Traditional Sicilian fare, artfully served
	HISTORY	Built in the 1970s as a hotel, the Atelier Sul Mare was transformed in the 1980s
	X-FACTOR	Being the living part of an artwork

Tapetenwechsel

Wenn Sie hier Gast sind, werden Sie sicher jede Nacht in einem anderen Zimmer verbringen wollen. Der tägliche Tapetenwechsel gehört im L'Atelier sul Mare zum guten Ton, denn die Gäste sollen so viel wie möglich von ihrem Aufenthalt in diesem einzigartigen Hotel profitieren können. Nur wenige Schritte vom Meer entfernt in einer der schönsten Buchten Siziliens an der Küste zwischen Palermo und Messina gelegen, verwirklicht dieses Hotel ein außergewöhnliches Konzept, bei dem die Gästezimmer gleichzeitig Ausstellungsräume sind. Viele Räume wurden von bekannten Künstlern gestaltet und tragen entsprechend der fantasievollen Interieurs poetische Namen: »Träume inmitten der Zeichnungen« hat die Entwicklung des Schreibens zum Thema, »Der Raum des Propheten« ist eine visuelle Hommage an den Regisseur Pier Paolo Pasolini und im »Turm von Sigismondo« hängt von der durchsichtigen Decke ein runder Turm herab, – darunter dreht sich ein riesiges Bett langsam im Kreise.

Dieses Haus wirkt eher wie ein Museum als wie ein Hotel, doch sein Gründer erklärt, dass »das Kunstwerk erst dann vollendet ist, wenn ein Besucher sich mit dem Raum auseinandersetzt und darin lebt. Die Nutzung der Räume ist integraler, ja unabdingbarer Aspekt der Werke.«

Buchtipps: »Der Leopard« von Giuseppe Tomasi di Lampedusa
»Pier Paolo Pasolini. Eine Biografie« von Nico Naldini

De chambre en chambre

À coup sûr, les clients de l' Atelier sul Mare voudront changer de chambre toutes les nuits ! Ici, les hôtes ont coutume de déménager chaque jour pour profiter au maximum de cet hôtel hors du commun. Situé entre Palerme et Messine, dans l'une des plus belles baies siciliennes et à seulement quelques pas de la mer, l'hôtel concrétise un concept inédit selon lequel chaque chambre est un objet d'art en soi. La plupart d'entre elles ont été créées par des artistes connus et sont dotées de noms poétiques à l'image de ces intérieurs originaux : celle des « Rêves parmi les dessins » s'inspire de l'évolution de l'écriture, « La Chambre du prophète » rend hommage au metteur en scène Pier Paolo Pasolini et dans « La tour de Sigismondo » une tour circulaire descend du plafond transparent. À son pied, un immense lit circulaire tourne lentement sur lui-même.

On pourrait se croire dans un musée plutôt que dans un hôtel, mais comme l'explique son créateur, « l'œuvre d'art n'est complète que lorsqu'un hôte a pénétré dans la chambre et y vit ; l'utilisation de la chambre forme une partie intégrante et fondamentale de l'œuvre. »

Livres à emporter: « Le Guépard » de Giuseppe Tomasi di Lampedusa
« Pier Paolo Pasolini : Biographie » de Nico Naldini

ANREISE	2 Fahrstunden westlich von Palermo, in der Nähe von Cefalù
Preis	Standardzimmer ab 54 €, Künstlerzimmer zwischen 80 und 90 €, inklusive Frühstück
ZIMMER	40 Zimmer und Suiten; 24 von jungen europäischen Künstlern gestaltete Standardzimmer, 14 von zeitgenössischen Künstlern gestaltete Zimmer
KÜCHE	Traditionelle sizilianische Gerichte, kunstvoll präsentiert
GESCHICHTE	1970 errichtet und in den 1980er-Jahren umgebaut
X-FAKTOR	Hier sind Sie lebender Bestandteil eines Kunstwerks

ACCÈS	À deux heures de route de Palerme, près de la ville de Cefalù
PRIX	Les chambres standard à partir de 54 €, les chambres artistiques de 80 à 90 €, petit déjeuner compris
CHAMBRES	40 chambres et suites ; 24 chambres standard, décorées par de jeunes artistes européens, 14 créées par des artistes contemporains
RESTAURATION	Cuisine sicilienne traditionnelle, servie avec art
HISTOIRE	Hôtel construit en 1970 et transformé dans les années 1980
LES « PLUS »	Devenir l'élément vivant d'une œuvre d'art

Style beacon...
Hotel Portixol, Mallorca

Hotel Portixol, Mallorca

Style beacon

Cool Swedish style transposed to a warm Mediterranean climate seems a near-perfect union. This pairing has given rise to the Hotel Portixol. Designed and built in 1956 by a Spanish architect, the Portixol was recently rescued from years of neglect and revitalized by its Swedish proprietors, who describe the hotel's style as "marine art deco". The white low-rise structure stands out against the deep blue Majorcan sky, like a cubed lighthouse watching over the harbour. Inside, it is a serene blend of Scandinavian and Spanish modernism. Some of the original 1950s furniture and fittings have been restored, but most of the interior is newly designed, complementing the classic clean lines of the architecture. The hotel's generously sized swimming pool and the sun lounges alongside it are original, re-established as a glamorous lounging place for guests.

Although one of this holiday island's many beaches is just a few metres from the hotel, and the atmospheric old town of Palma is only a short walk away, it would be understandable if visitors to the Portixol chose to stay within its elegant walls.

Books to pack: "A Winter in Majorca" by George Sand "Tamara de Lempicka: A Life of Deco and Decadence" by Laura Claridge

Hotel Portixol
Calle Sirena 27
07006 Palma de Mallorca
Spain
Tel: + 34 971 27 18 00
Fax: + 34 971 27 50 25
E-mail: hotel@portixol.com
Website: www.portixol.com

DIRECTIONS	1.5 km/1 m from Palma de Mallorca
RATES	€ 110 to 325, breakfast included
ROOMS	23 rooms, including suites
FOOD	This restaurant is especially renowned for its seafood
HISTORY	Built and opened in 1956, modernized in 1999
X-FACTOR	Style and sun

Das kommt mir schwedisch vor

Kühler schwedischer Stil in warmem, mediterranem Klima – eine traumhafte Kombination, die Sie im Hotel Portixol verwirklicht finden. Dieses 1956 von einem spanischen Architekten entworfene Hotel wurde erst kürzlich von den jetzigen schwedischen Besitzern vor dem Verfall gerettet und renoviert. Den Stil des Portixol bezeichnen die neuen Hausherren als »maritimes Art déco«. Das flache, weiße Gebäude, das sich gegen den tiefblauen Himmel über Mallorca abhebt, wacht wie ein kubischer Leuchtturm über den Hafen. Das Innere des Hauses besticht durch eine heitere Mischung aus skandinavischem und spanischem Modernismus. Einige der Originalmöbel und -einrichtungen aus den 1950er-Jahren hat man restaurieren lassen, aber der Großteil der Interieurs wurde in Abstimmung auf die klassischen, klaren Linien der Architektur neu entworfen. Der großzügige Pool des Hotels und die zugehörigen Sonnenliegen wurden als stilvolle Oase, in der sich Gäste des Hauses entspannen können, original erhalten. Obwohl das Haus nur wenige Meter von einem der zahlreichen Strände der Ferieninsel und gerade einmal zwei Kilometer von der stimmungsvollen Altstadt von Palma entfernt liegt, ist es nur zu verständlich, wenn Besucher die eleganten Räume des Hotel Portixol vorziehen sollten.

**Buchtipps: »Ein Winter auf Mallorca« von George Sand
»Tamara de Lempicka. Ein Leben für Dekor und Dekadenz« von Laura Claridge**

Une touche suédoise dans un décor méditerranéen

Dans une combinaison proche de la perfection, l'hôtel Portixol associe l'élégance discrète du style suédois et la chaleur méditerranéenne. Dessiné et construit en 1956 par un architecte espagnol, puis laissé à l'abandon durant de longues années, le Portixol a été repris en main par ses propriétaires suédois qui qualifient son style « d'Art Déco marin ». Sa basse silhouette blanche se détache sur le bleu éclatant du ciel de Majorque tel un phare en forme de cube qui veillerait sur le port. L'intérieur est un mélange harmonieux de modernisme scandinave et espagnol. Certains éléments du mobilier et des installations des années 1950 ont été restaurés, mais l'intérieur a été en grande partie réaménagé et complète les lignes sobres et classiques de l'architecture. La vaste piscine et le solarium, construits en même temps que l'hôtel, ont été luxueusement rénovés et forment un cadre élégant pour la détente.

Bien que l'une des nombreuses plages de l'île touristique ne se trouve qu'à quelques mètres de l'hôtel, et la vieille ville animée de Palma à deux kilomètres seulement, on ne pourrait s'étonner que les hôtes du Portixol préfèrent ne pas quitter son décor raffiné.

Livre à emporter: « Un Hiver à Majorque » de George Sand

ANREISE	1,5 km von Palma de Mallorca entfernt
PREIS	Zwischen 110 und 325 €, Frühstück inklusive
ZIMMER	23 Zimmer und Suiten
KÜCHE	Vor allem für seine Meeresfrüchte berühmtes Restaurant
GESCHICHTE	Gebaut und eröffnet 1956, modernisiert 1999
X-FAKTOR	Stil und Sonne

ACCÈS	À 1,5 km de Palma de Majorque
PRIX	De 110 à 325 €, petit déjeuner compris
CHAMBRES	23 chambres et suites
RESTAURATION	Restaurant réputé, en particulier pour ses fruits de mer
HISTOIRE	Construit et ouvert en 1956, modernisé en 1999
LES « PLUS »	Raffinement et soleil

Silence is golden...
Finca Son Gener, Mallorca

Finca Son Gener,
Mallorca

Silence is golden

Rural life has many rewards; one of the best is silence. And although the crowing of a rooster or the bleating of sheep may break that silence now and then, the peace and quiet that rules here is a treat in our noisy world.

On the island of Majorca, there is the chance to lead a simple country life for a few days. Some of the most beautiful places here are set in idyllic landscapes just near the coast, and often hidden behind thick natural stone walls. The country estate of Son Gener is one of these havens. Built in the 18th century, and used for making oils and grains, it has been totally restored. The classic finca – farm – is on the eastern side of the island, on the brow of a small hill, with a view of the village, sea, and mountains. Surrounded by green fields, olive and almond trees, this is a dream domain to bask in. While the estate's simple style is in keeping with its tranquil backdrop, it has been refurbished with skill. The soft rich colours that make up the interiors are in themselves conducive to a sense of calm. The elegant house calls to mind the patrician life of past days. Those who are privileged to be guests here will be content with their choice for a pastoral interlude.

Book to pack: "Goya" by Lion Feuchtwanger

Finca Son Gener	
Apartat de Correus, 136	
07550 Son Servera	
Majorca	
Spain	
Tel: + 34 971 183612	
Fax: + 34 971 183591	
E-mail: rustic@mallorcaonline.com	
No website	

DIRECTIONS	Between the towns of Son Servera and Artà, 70 km/44 m east from Palma de Mallorca, 20 km/12 m northeast from Manacor
RATES	Each suite from € 222, including breakfast
ROOMS	10 suites
FOOD	On request, Majorcan dishes made with homegrown organic produce are served
HISTORY	Built in the 18th century, the finca was turned into a hotel in 1998
X-FACTOR	Outdoor and indoor serenity

Himmlische Ruhe

Das Landleben hat viele Vorzüge, aber einer der größten ist die Stille. Und auch wenn sie gelegentlich durch das Krähen eines Hahns oder das Blöken eines Schafs unterbrochen wird, herrscht doch meist Ruhe und Frieden – ein Luxus in unserer lauten Welt.

Auf der Insel Mallorca haben Sie Gelegenheit, für einige Tage dem einfachen Landleben zu frönen. Einige der schönsten Unterkünfte finden sich hier inmitten idyllischer Landschaften nahe der Küste, oft versteckt hinter dicken Mauern aus Naturstein. Unter ihnen ist auch der Landsitz von Son Gener, eine klassische Finca, wie hier die Bauern-höfe genannt werden, die auf der Ostseite der Insel auf der Kuppe eines kleinen Hügels liegt. Umgeben von grünen Feldern, Olivenhainen und Mandelbäumen finden Sie hier ein traumhaftes Urlaubsziel. Das im 18. Jahrhundert ursprünglich für die Öl- und Getreideproduktion gebaute Haus wurde komplett und mit großem Können renoviert. Davon zeugt der einfache Stil des Hauses, welcher sich harmonisch in die Umgebung einpasst. Zur allgemeinen Atmosphäre der Ruhe tragen die sanften, satten Farben im Hausinneren bei. Das elegante Haus weckt Erinnerungen an das Leben des gehobenen Bürgertums in früheren Zeiten. Wer das Privileg genießt, an diesem Ort Gast zu sein, wird mit seiner Wahl dieser ländlichen Oase der Ruhe mehr als zufrieden sein.

Buchtipp: »Goya oder der arge Weg der Erkenntnis« von Lion Feuchtwanger

Le silence est d'or

La vie à la campagne a de nombreux avantages, en particulier le silence. Dans notre monde bruyant, cette paix et cette tranquillité, seulement interrompues de temps à autre par le cri d'un coq ou le bêlement d'un mouton, constituent un plaisir authentique.

Dans l'île de Majorque, on peut, le temps d'un séjour, goûter à la vie campagnarde simple. Ici, certaines des plus belles villégiatures se cachent souvent derrière d'épais murs de pierre, dans des cadres idylliques, à proximité du littoral. Le domaine de Son Gener est l'un de ces havres de paix. Construit au XVIIIᵉ siècle, à l'origine destiné au pressage de l'huile et à la culture des céréales, il a été entièrement restauré. Cette finca (ferme) traditionnelle est située dans la partie orientale de l'île, au sommet d'une petite colline. Entourée de champs verdoyants, d'oliviers et d'amandiers, c'est un lieu de détente rêvé. Si le style simple du domaine s'harmonise avec son cadre rustique, celui-ci a été rénové avec goût. Les couleurs riches et douces des intérieurs favo-risent l'impression de sérénité. L'élégante maison principale évoque la vie patricienne d'antan.

Les privilégiés qui auront la chance de séjourner à Son Gener seront ravis du choix de leur interlude champêtre.

Livre à emporter : « Goya » de Lion Feuchtwanger

ANREISE	Zwischen den Städten Son Servera und Artà, 70 km östlich von Palma, 20 km nordöstlich von Manacor
PREIS	Suiten inklusive Frühstück ab 222 €
ZIMMER	10 Suiten
KÜCHE	Auf Anfrage werden inseltypische Gerichte mit Zutaten aus eigenem biologischem Anbau serviert
GESCHICHTE	Das Gebäude stammt aus dem 18. Jahrhundert und ist seit 1998 Hotel
X-FAKTOR	Entspannte Atmosphäre in Haus und Umgebung

ACCÈS	Entre les villes de Son Servera et Artà, à 70 km à l'est de Palma, à 20 km au nord-est de Manacor
PRIX	Chaque suite, petit déjeuner compris, à partir de 222 €
CHAMBRES	10 suites
RESTAURATION	Sur demande, plats majorquins préparés avec des produits bio cultivés sur place
HISTOIRE	Construit au XVIIIᵉ siècle, le bâtiment est un hôtel depuis 1998
LES « PLUS »	Sérénité intérieure et extérieure

Monasterio romántico...
Monasterio Rocamador, Extremadura

Monasterio Rocamador, Extremadura

Monasterio romántico

This striking structure has crowned this hilltop in rural Spain since the 16th century. Although it looks like a small village, it was once a monastery and then a centre of philosophy.

Its most recent reincarnation is as a hotel. Rocamador is a respite for fugitives from a hectic life; at a pace far less serene than the monastic one. Although the furnishing of the guestrooms is simple, they are anything but cell-like in their comforts.

The restaurant, converted from what was once the chapel, is not at all austere in its menu. It proffers cuisine of a superior standard to that which the brothers would have been served. With no set schedule to abide by, guests can spend all the time they like beside or in the infinity pool; play pelota or go horseriding, before enjoying nights of blessed repose after a divine dinner.

On the other hand, this quiet region is known as the "land of the conquistadors". Its rich landscape, dotted with grand castles, chestnut forests, and whitewashed towns, is one that lures the explorer. Expeditions in search of the leather and crafts that the area is known for will bring certain rewards.

Books to pack: "The Consolations of Philosophy" by Alain de Botton

"Raquel, the Jewess of Toledo" by Lion Feuchtwanger

Monasterio Rocamador		
Apdo. Correos n.7		
Barcarrota		
06160 Badajoz		
Extremadura		
Spain		
Tel: + 34 924 489 000		
Fax: +34 924 489 000		
E-mail: mail@rocamador.com		
Website: www.rocamador.com		

DIRECTIONS	40 km/25 m south-east from Badajoz, near the border of Spain and Portugal	
RATES	From € 102 to 210	
ROOMS	30 rooms	
FOOD	One of Spain's most talked-about restaurants	
HISTORY	Built in the 16th century, the monastery was opened as a hotel in 1997	
X-FACTOR	A truly romantic hermitage	

Klösterliche Romantik

Bereits im 16. Jahrhundert wurde dieser eindrucksvolle Bau inmitten der hügeligen, ländlichen Landschaft der spanischen Extremadura erbaut. Aus dem einstigen Kloster, das fast wie ein eigenes kleines Dorf wirkt, wurde später ein reges geistiges Zentrum.

In jüngster Zeit machte das Rocamador wieder eine Wandlung durch – diesmal in ein Hotel, das Zuflucht vor dem hektischen Alltagsleben bietet, auch wenn ihm längst nicht mehr die klösterliche Stille innewohnt wie damals. Obwohl die Zimmer sehr einfach ausgestattet sind, liegt der Komfort weit über dem einer Mönchszelle. Auch das Essen im Restaurant, das sich dort befindet, wo früher die Kapelle war, ist alles andere als asketisch. Die Speisen, die dort serviert werden, sind von weitaus höherer Qualität als das, was zu Zeiten der Ordensbrüder auf den Tisch kam. Auch müssen die Gäste hier keinem strengen Zeitplan folgen, sondern können nach Lust und Laune am riesigen Swimmingpool liegen, Pelota spielen oder reiten, um sich schließlich nach einem göttlichen Essen der seligen Nachtruhe hinzugeben. Jedoch ist diese ruhige Gegend auch als das »Land der Konquistadoren« bekannt. Die eindrucksvolle, mit Burgen übersäte Landschaft, die Kastanienwälder und die weiß getünchten Städte waren eine große Verlockung für die Eroberer. Die Expeditionen, die Sie unternehmen, um Lederwaren oder Kunsthandwerk zu erlangen, werden gewiss von Erfolg gekrönt sein.

Buchtipps: »Trost der Philosophie. Eine Gebrauchsanweisung« von Alain de Botton
»Die Jüdin von Toledo« von Lion Feuchtwanger

Monasterio romántico

Cet ouvrage impressionnant fut construit au XVIe siècle au cœur de la campagne vallonnée de l'Extramadura. L'ancien monastère aux allures de village devint plus tard un centre spirituel animé.

Récemment reconverti en hôtel, Rocamador est aujourd'hui un refuge pour tout ceux qui désirent fuir les trépidations d'une vie bien moins sereine que l'existence monacale. Bien que meublées avec simplicité, les chambres sont confortables et ne ressemblent plus en rien à des cellules. Installé dans l'ancienne chapelle, le restaurant est de même dénué d'austérité : il propose une cuisine fort supérieure à celle dont devaient se satisfaire les moines. Entièrement libres de leur temps, les hôtes peuvent se prélasser à leur guise au bord de la piscine, jouer à la pelota ou randonner à cheval, avant de savourer un dîner divin, suivi du plus doux des sommeils.

Cette région si paisible est aussi connue pour être le « pays des conquistadors ». Ses superbes paysages émaillés d'imposants châteaux, de forêts de marronniers et de villages blanchis à la chaux, incitent à la découverte. On fera également de bonnes trouvailles si l'on s'intéresse à l'artisanat et aux articles de cuir pour lesquels l'endroit est réputé.

Livres à emporter : « Les Consolations de la philosophie » d'Alain de Botton
« La Juive de Tolède » de Lion Feuchtwanger

ANREISE	40 km südöstlich von Badajoz, nahe der spanisch-portugiesischen Grenze
PREIS	Zwischen 102 und 210 €
ZIMMER	30 Zimmer
KÜCHE	Eines der meist gepriesenen Restaurants Spaniens
GESCHICHTE	Im 16. Jahrhundert erbaut, seit 1997 als Hotel in Betrieb
X-FAKTOR	Stilvolle Auszeit

ACCÈS	À 40 km au sud-est de Badajoz, près de la frontière du Portugal
PRIX	De 102 à 210 €
CHAMBRES	30 chambres
RESTAURATION	L'une des tables les plus réputées d'Espagne
HISTOIRE	Bâtiment construit au XVIe siècle, converti en hôtel en 1997
LES « PLUS »	Un cadre hors du temps

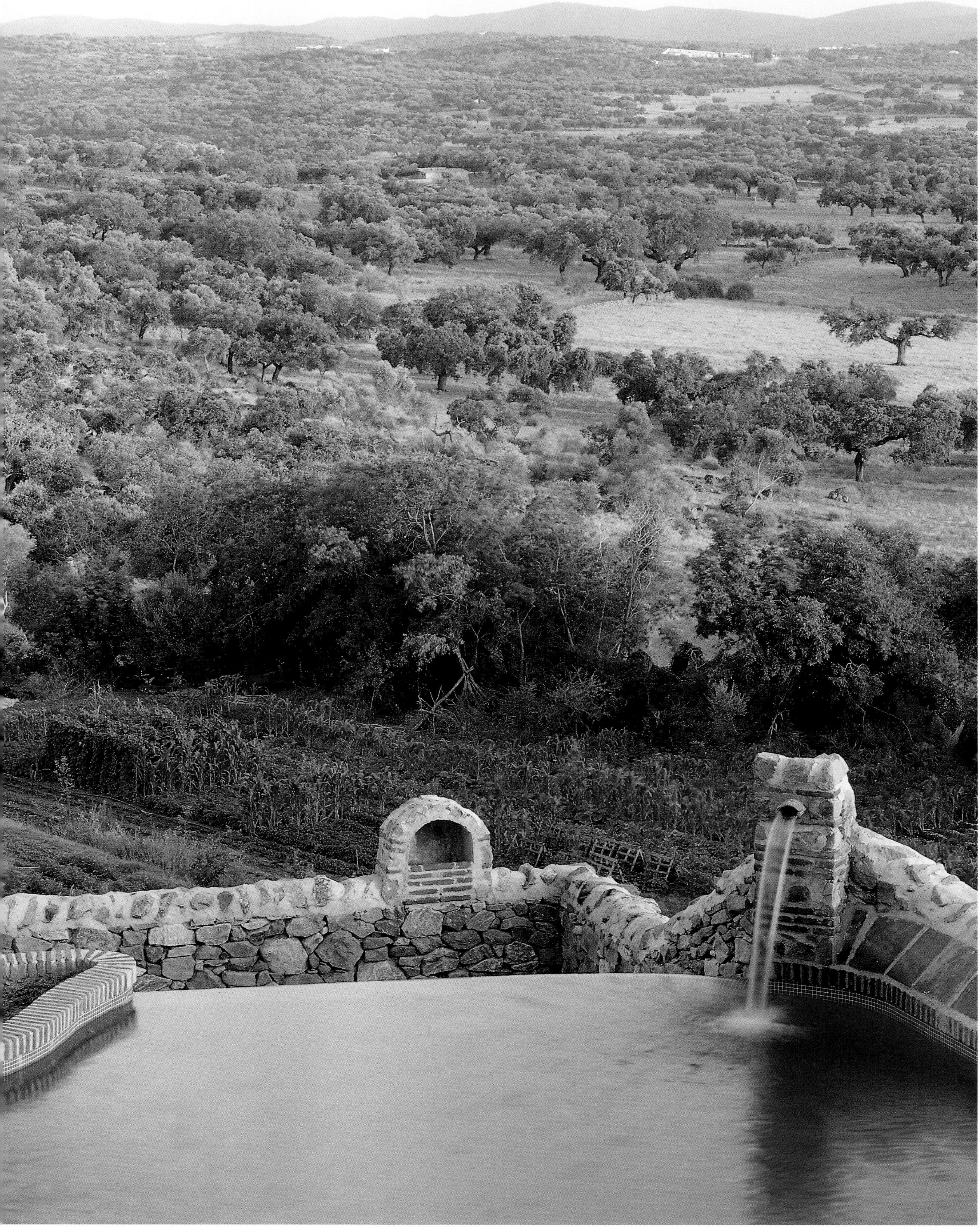

Noble sacrifice...
Casa de Carmona, Sevilla

Casa de Carmona, Sevilla

Noble sacrifice

For a few days, live as though you were a Spanish aristocrat. If you are one already, you'll feel right at home here. Those who take care of you at Casa de Carmona, a palace now transformed into a fine hotel, will let you pretend – for a while. When you pass through the massive door of this 16th-century house, one that was home for more than four hundred years to one dynasty, you are back in nobler times. It will be easy to grow used to living in these lavish surroundings. And no doubt you will soon become accustomed to the splendid food. While others tend to the chores, you will be free to breathe in the fresh mountain air, survey the gardens, and rest in the courtyards, shaded from the sunlight. Your tasks will be to inhale the scent of the orange trees and the jasmine; listen to the silence, the murmur of the fountains, and the singing of the birds.

The palace is in the heart of the town of Carmona, said to be one of the oldest settlements in Spain. It has seen the rise and fall of successive empires. As a result, some of the most stunning Roman and Renaissance architecture in the country is to be found here.

Book to pack: "Don Quixote" by Miguel de Cervantes

Casa de Carmona
Plaza de Lazzo, 1
Carmona
41410 Seville
Spain
Tel: + 34 954 191 000
Fax: + 34 954 190 189
E-mail: reserve@casacarmona.com
Website: www.casadecarmona.com

DIRECTIONS	About 37 km/23 m east of Seville
RATES	Rooms € 190 to 300, Suite € 750 to 1000
ROOMS	31 rooms, 1 suite
FOOD	Traditional Spanish cuisine with a contemporary twist
HISTORY	The Casa was built in 1561. Renovated between 1986 and 1991 it has been a hotel since then
X-FACTOR	Leading the lifestyle of a lord and lady

Ein nobles Opfer

Leben Sie ein paar Tage wie ein spanischer Adliger!
Das äußerst zuvorkommende Personal der Casa de Carmona,
eines ehemaligen Palasts, der in ein Hotel umgewandelt
wurde, wird Sie – wenigstens für kurze Zeit – darin unter-
stützen. Wenn Sie durch das mächtige Portal des aus dem
16. Jahrhundert stammenden Prachtbaus treten, der mehr
als vierhundert Jahre von einem Adelsgeschlecht bewohnt
wurde, werden Sie sich sogleich in größere Zeiten zurück-
versetzt fühlen. Gewiss wird es Ihnen nicht schwer fallen,
sich in diesem luxuriösen Ambiente einzuleben, und auch
an das köstliche Essen werden Sie sich sehr bald gewöhnen.
Während die anderen die Hausarbeit erledigen, können Sie
in den Bergen die gute Luft genießen, die Gärten bewundern oder sich im schattigen Innenhof entspannen. Ihre
einzige Pflicht besteht darin, den Duft der Orangenbäume
und Jasmine einzuatmen und der Stille, dem leisen
Plätschern des Brunnens und dem Zwitschern der Vögel
zu lauschen.
Der Palast liegt im Herzen der Stadt Carmona, einer der
ältesten Ortschaften Spaniens, die noch heute von der Blüte
und dem Untergang aufeinander folgender Königreiche
zeugt. Hier befinden sich die schönsten Bauwerke der
Romanik und der Renaissance von ganz Spanien.
Buchtipp: »Don Quijote« von Miguel de Cervantes

Noblesse oblige

Offrez-vous le luxe, pendant quelques jours, de vivre à la
manière d'un aristocrate espagnol. Si vous appartenez à la
noblesse, alors vous vous sentirez ici comme chez vous.
Vos hôtes de la Casa de Carmona, un palais transformé en
hôtel de luxe, vous donneront le change... le temps d'un court
séjour. À peine aurez-vous franchi la porte massive de cette
demeure du XVIe siècle, qui a abrité une seule dynastie pendant plus de quatre cents ans, que vous vous croirez trans-
porté à l'époque des seigneurs. Mais vous vous adapterez
sans aucun doute rapidement à l'environnement luxueux, et
plus encore à la cuisine succulente. Tandis que le personnel
s'affaire, libre à vous de flâner dans les jardins ou de vous
reposer dans les cours ombragées en respirant l'air frais des
montagnes. Votre tâche se limitera à inhaler le parfum des
orangers et des jasmins, ou encore à écouter le silence, le
murmure des fontaines et le chant des oiseaux.
Le palais est situé au cœur de Carmona, l'une des plus
vieilles villes d'Espagne. Témoin de la grandeur et de la
décadence de plusieurs empires, cette cité abrite quelques-
unes des plus belles architectures de style roman et
Renaissance du pays.
Livre à emporter : « Don Quichotte » de Miguel de Cervantès

ANREISE	Etwa 37 km östlich von Sevilla
PREIS	Zimmer zwischen 190 und 300 €, Suite zwischen 750 und 1000 €
ZIMMER	31 Zimmer und 1 Suite
KÜCHE	Traditionelle spanische Küche mit modernem Einschlag
GESCHICHTE	Die Casa wurde 1561 erbaut. Nach ihrer Renovierung von 1986 und 1991 wurde sie als Hotel eröffnet
X-FAKTOR	Leben wie ein Edelmann oder eine Edelfrau

ACCÈS	À 37 km environ à l'est de Séville
PRIX	Chambres de 190 à 300 €, suite de 750 à 1000 €
CHAMBRES	31 chambres et 1 suite
RESTAURATION	Cuisine traditionnelle espagnole, aux accents contemporains
HISTOIRE	La Casa a été construite en 1561 et reconvertie en hôtel après une rénovation de 1986 à 1991
LES « PLUS »	Vivre en grand seigneur

An island on an island...
Hotel San Roque, Teneriffa

Hotel San Roque, Tenerife

An island on an island

The Tenerife village of Garachico is a one-hotel town. Fortunately, that hotel is the San Roque, once a private mansion, now a peaceful sanctuary for travellers.

Here, traditional and contemporary elements have been cleverly melded into one stylish whole. In the centre of the atmospheric old courtyard, an impressive steel sculpture points upwards at the ever-present sun. Each of the guest rooms is different, although all are furnished with classic pieces from famous designers such as Le Corbusier, Mies van de Rohe, Eileen Gray, and Charles Rennie Mackintosh. Whether you choose to read a book in a shady corner of the courtyard, bask in the sun by the pool, or watch the sunset from the roof patio, you will make yourself at home here. You can visit the peaceful village and the nearby beaches, or hike in the bizarre volcanic countryside and the Teno Mountains. If you prefer peace and quiet, you can experience all the rest and relaxation you need within the ambience of the Hotel San Roque's walls.

Books to pack: "From Bauhaus to Our House" by Tom Wolfe "Blood Wedding" by Federico Garcia Lorca

Hotel San Roque
Esteban de Ponte 32
38450 Garachico
Tenerife
Spain
Tel: + 34 (0) 922 1334 35
Fax : + 34 (0) 922 1334 06
E-mail: info@hotelsanroque.com
Website: www.hotelsanroque.com

DIRECTIONS	On Tenerife's northwest coast, an hour's drive from Reina Sofia's Airport on Tenerife
RATES	€ 130 to 300 per person, including breakfast
ROOMS	20 rooms, including 4 suites
FOOD	Dine on local cuisine at the hotel restaurant and local cafes
HISTORY	Built in the 17th century Hotel San Roque was opened as a hotel in 1997
X-FACTOR	Contemporary art teamed with historic surroundings

Eine Insel auf der Insel

Das Dorf Garachico auf Teneriffa besitzt nur ein einziges Hotel. Glücklicherweise handelt es sich dabei um das Hotel San Roque, eine herrschaftliche Villa, die sich einst in Privatbesitz befand, heute aber ein ruhiges Plätzchen für Reisende ist.

Hier ist es gelungen, traditionelle und moderne Elemente zu einer Einheit zusammenzufügen. Inmitten des stimmungsvollen, alten Innenhofs steht eine eindrucksvolle Stahlplastik, die zur allgegenwärtigen Sonne weist. Die Gästezimmer sind alle unterschiedlich, obwohl sie sämtlich mit Möbeln berühmter Designer wie Le Corbusier, Mies van der Rohe, Eileen Gray und Charles Rennie Mackintosh ausgestattet sind. Egal ob Sie sich entscheiden, in einem schattigen Winkel des Innenhofs ein Buch zu lesen oder sich am Swimmingpool in der Sonne zu aalen oder von der Dachterrasse aus den Sonnenuntergang zu beobachten, Sie werden sich hier zu Hause fühlen. Alternativ kann man auch das friedliche Dorf und die nahe gelegenen Strände besuchen oder in der bizarren Vulkanlandschaft und dem Teno-Gebirge wandern gehen.

Wenn Sie die absolute Stille suchen, sind Sie im San Roque Hotel goldrichtig, denn hier finden Sie so viel Entspannung und Ruhe, wie Ihnen lieb ist.

Buchtipps: »Mit dem Bauhaus leben« von Tom Wolfe
»Bluthochzeit« von Federico Garcia Lorca

Une oasis de paix sur une île

Le village de Garachico, sur l'île de Tenerife, n'abrite qu'un hôtel. Par bonheur, cet hôtel est le San Roque, une ancienne résidence privée transformée en sanctuaire pour voyageurs en quête de tranquillité.

Ici, le traditionnel et le contemporain se conjuguent harmonieusement pour former un ensemble de grande classe. Au centre de la pittoresque cour, une impressionnante sculpture en acier s'élance vers le soleil omniprésent. Chaque chambre est différente, mais toutes sont dotées de meubles signés, notamment Le Corbusier, Mies van der Rohe, Eileen Gray et Charles Rennie Mackintosh. Que vous souhaitiez lire dans un coin ombragé de la cour, vous faire dorer près de la piscine ou admirer le coucher du soleil depuis la terrasse du toit, vous vous sentirez aussi à l'aise que chez vous. Vous pouvez visiter le village paisible et les plages des environs, à moins que vous ne préfériez randonner dans l'étonnant paysage volcanique ou les montagnes Teno.

Si vous préférez le repos complet, vous trouverez entre les murs de l'hôtel San Roque un véritable havre de paix.

Livre à emporter: « Ferias : Poèmes inédits » de Federico Garcia Lorca

ANREISE	An der Nordwestküste Teneriffas, eine Autostunde vom Flughafen Reina Sofia entfernt gelegen	ACCÈS	Sur la côte nord-ouest de Tenerife, à une heure de route de l'aéroport Reina Sofia
PREIS	Zwischen 130 und 300 € pro Person, Frühstück inklusive	PRIX	De 130 à 300 € par personne, petit déjeuner compris
ZIMMER	20 Zimmer inklusive 4 Suiten	CHAMBRES	20 chambres, dont 4 suites
KÜCHE	Lokale Küche im Hotelrestaurant und in den Cafés am Ort	RESTAURATION	Cuisine régionale dans le restaurant de l'hôtel et les cafés avoisinants
GESCHICHTE	Erbaut im 17. Jahrhundert, als Hotel geöffnet seit 1997	HISTOIRE	Construit au XVIIe siècle, l'hôtel a ouvert en 1997
X-FAKTOR	Zeitgenössische Kunst in historischem Ambiente	LES « PLUS »	Art contemporain et site historique

This glorious Eden...
Quinta da Capela, Sintra

Quinta da Capela, Sintra

This glorious Eden
Some of the most famous talkers have had something to say about the town of Sintra. Its virtues have been extolled by poets and writers. For centuries the lovely village was the summer refuge of the royalty of Portugal. Keen to escape the stifling heat of the city, the rest of the nobility came here too. Grand residences were built so that the peers of the realm could holiday in the style to which they were accustomed. Many were set just beyond the town, out in the country, for more peace and quiet. Lush gardens and thick walls thwarted prying eyes.
One of the palatial homes is Quinta da Capela, which is now an aristocratic guesthouse; one with a more modest lineage. It has an exterior that steers clear of decoration. But behind the simple façade there is an elegant interior with high vaulted ceilings, expansive rooms, and wide doors that look out on lush greenery. A discreet and refined sense of luxury is apparent in the very simplicity of the furnishings. Lord Byron would have liked it, especially the classic garden with its peacocks and swans. It was he, hard to please, who called Sintra "perhaps the most delightful place in Europe".
Books to pack: "Fernando Pessoa & Co: Selected Poems" ed. by Richard Zenith
"Byron: Child of Passion, Fool of Fame" by Benita Eisler

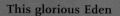

Quinta da Capela		
Monserrate Sintra	DIRECTIONS	30 km/19 m northwest of Lisbon; 4 km/2.4 m from the centre of Sintra
Sintra 2710	RATES	Rooms and Suites from € 130 to 185, including breakfast; apartments from € 185 to 320. Closed between November and March
Portugal		
Tel: + 351 21 9290170		
Fax: + 351 21 9293425	ROOMS	7 in the main house, and 3 cottages in the grounds
No e-mail	FOOD	There is a restaurant 5 minutes drive from the Quinta
No website	HISTORY	The first Quinta was built in the 16th century but was destroyed in the great Lisbon earthquake of 1755. It was rebuilt in 1773 and opened as a hotel in the 1980s
	X-FACTOR	Historical atmosphere with beautiful surroundings

Hier liegt das Paradies

Nicht wenige berühmte Dichter und Denker haben Sintra in ihren Werken Denkmäler gesetzt. Über Hunderte von Jahren war hier die Sommerresidenz des portugiesischen Königshauses. Ihm auf den Fersen folgte der Adel, der ebenfalls der drückenden Hitze der Stadt entkommen wollte. Die Hochwohlgeborenen des Reiches ließen sich prachtvolle Residenzen errichten, um auch im Urlaub nicht auf den gewohnten Lebensstil verzichten zu müssen. Oft befanden sich diese direkt vor der Stadt, doch dabei schon mitten auf dem Land, und boten Ruhe und Frieden. Vor neugierigen Blicken schützten üppige Gärten und dicke Mauern.

Auch Quinta da Capela war einst ein solcher Palast. Heute beherbergt er ein nicht minder aristokratisches Gästehaus, was sich jedoch in angenehmer Zurückhaltung ausdrückt. Das Äußere des Palasts verzichtet ganz auf dekorative Elemente. Hinter der einfachen Fassade verbirgt sich ein elegantes Inneres: hohe Bogendecken, weite Türen und großzügige Räume, die auf prächtiges Gartengrün blicken. Diskret-raffinierter Luxus wird auch bei der Einrichtung spürbar: Das Mobiliar ist bewusst einfach gehalten. Lord Byron hätte es hier gefallen. Besonders beeindruckt hätte ihn sicher der im klassischen Stil angelegte Garten, in dem sich Pfaue und Schwäne tummeln. Denn er, der bekanntermaßen nicht leicht zufrieden zu stellen war, bezeichnete Sintra einst als »den wohl schönsten Flecken in ganz Europa«.

Buchtipps: »Esoterische Gedichte« von Fernando Pessoa »Byron. Der Held im Kostüm« von Benita Eisler

Un petit coin de paradis

Sintra a inspiré certains de nos plus grands orateurs, et ses vertus ont été vantées par maints écrivains et poètes. Des siècles durant, cette charmante petite ville servit de retraite estivale à la famille royale du Portugal. Désireuse d'échapper à l'accablante chaleur de la ville, la noblesse y venait également pendant les mois d'été. De luxueuses résidences furent édifiées pour que les pairs du royaume villégiaturent dans le style auquel ils étaient accoutumés. Beaucoup furent construites à l'extérieur de la localité, dans la campagne qui offrait plus de silence et de tranquillité. De luxuriants jardins et des murs épais protégeaient des regards curieux.

L'une de ces résidences est la Quinta da Capela, aujourd'hui convertie en un hôtel aussi sobre qu'élégant. Derrière une façade dépourvue de tout ornement, se cache un intérieur d'un grand raffinement. Sous les hauts plafonds voûtés, de vastes salles et de larges portes donnent sur une nature verdoyante. De la sobriété du mobilier se dégage un luxe à la fois chic et discret. Lord Byron aurait fort apprécié cet endroit, notamment le jardin classique peuplé de paons et de cygnes. C'est d'ailleurs cet hôte exigeant qui qualifia Sintra de « peut-être l'endroit le plus délicieux d'Europe ».

Livres à emporter : « Œuvres poétiques » de Fernando Pessoa « Lord Byron » de Gilbert Martineau

ANREISE	30 km nordwestlich von Lissabon; 4 km von Sintra entfernt
PREIS	Zimmer und Suiten zwischen 130 und 185 €, inklusive Frühstück; Apartments zwischen 185 und 320 €. Von November bis März geschlossen
ZIMMER	7 im Haupthaus, 3 Cottages auf dem Anwesen
KÜCHE	Restaurant in 5 Minuten Fahrt zu erreichen
GESCHICHTE	Erstmals erbaut im 16. Jahrhundert; nach der Zerstörung 1755 beim großen Lissaboner Erdbeben 1773 wiederaufgebaut. Als Hotel eröffnet seit den 1980er-Jahren
X-FAKTOR	Historisches Flair in wunderschöner Umgebung

ACCÈS	À 30 km au nord-ouest de Lisbonne et 4 km de Sintra
PRIX	Chambres et suites de 130 à 185 €, petit déjeuner compris, appartements de 185 à 320 €; fermé de novembre à mars
CHAMBRES	7 chambres dans le bâtiment principal, et 3 cottages dans le parc
RESTAURATION	Il y a un restaurant à 5 minutes de route de la Quinta
HISTOIRE	Construite au XVIe siècle, la Quinta a été détruite pendant le grand tremblement de terre à Lisbonne en 1755, rebâtie en 1773 et transformée en hôtel dans les années 1980
LES « PLUS »	Atmosphère historique dans un beau paysage

Somewhere in time...
Palace Hotel da Curia, Tamengos

Palace Hotel da Curia, Tamengos

Somewhere in time

In the 1920s, this was a splendid new hotel. One of the last grand Art Nouveau buildings in Europe, it was quite the most stylish place when it first welcomed guests through its doors. It was set in magnificent gardens, in an elegant Portuguese spa town; one to which high-society people came to take the so-called healing waters. Luckily, the Palace Hotel da Curia is as lovely now as it was back then. Time seems to have stood still here. The atmosphere is much as it used to be. Although it has been restored, you can see what it must have been like over half a century ago. Wisely, little has been changed; it has been kept looking much as it did in the old days. New comforts have been added, but all the chic of that golden era remains. Yet this stately old hotel is still a new landmark in a region that is steeped in history.

The Beiras by the Atlantic Coast is a less well-known part of Portugal; a part that is "off the beaten track". On the western coast, it is one of the most varied areas of the country. Its boundaries range from the mountains to the lush valleys, and from quiet villages to long curves of beach.

Book to pack: "Journey to Portugal" by José Saramago

Palace Hotel da Curia
Curia 3780-541
Tamengos
Portugal
Tel: + 351 231 510 300
Fax: +351 231 515 31
E-mail: curia@almeidahotels.com
Website: www.almeidahotels.com

DIRECTIONS	20 km/12 m north of Coimbra; 2 hours north from Lisbon, and an hour south from Porto
RATES	€ 75 to 90, inclusive of breakfast
ROOMS	114 rooms
FOOD	Local specialities and classic international cuisine
HISTORY	Built in the early 1920s, the Palace Hotel da Curia opened in 1926
X-FACTOR	Belle Époque flair

Eine andere Zeit

Erbaut in den 1920er-Jahren, gehörte das Hotel zu den letzten großen Jugendstilbauten Europas und galt, als es seine ersten Gäste willkommen hieß, als Verkörperung wahren Stils. Es lag in einer prachtvollen Gartenanlage, in einem eleganten Kurort, wo sich die High Society an den heilenden Quellen labte. Glücklicherweise scheint im Palace Hotel da Curia die Zeit stehen geblieben zu sein, sodass man förmlich die zauberhafte Atmosphäre vergangener Tage spürt. Obwohl das Hotel inzwischen renoviert wurde, kann man sich genau vorstellen, wie es hier vor mehr als einem halben Jahrhundert zuging. Denn es wurde klugerweise nur wenig verändert. Natürlich ist moderner Komfort hinzugekommen, doch der Flair des Goldenen Zeitalters blieb erhalten. Und man darf eines nicht vergessen: Inmitten dieser durch und durch historischen Landschaft ist das ehrwürdige alte Hotel immer noch ein relativ neues Wahrzeichen.

Die Landschaft Beiras an der Atlantikküste Portugals gehört zu den weniger bekannten Regionen, in die sich nicht jeder »verirrt«. Dabei ist sie eine der abwechslungsreichsten des Landes. Hier finden sich Bergzüge neben üppig begrünten Tälern, stille Dörfchen und lange Strände.

Buchtipp: »Hoffnung im Alentejo« von José Saramago

Réminiscences

Dans les années 1920, c'était un hôtel Art nouveau flambant neuf; l'un de ces établissements élégants où se côtoyait l'élite européenne. Entouré d'un magnifique jardin, il se dressait dans une ville portugaise alors très sélect, réputée pour ses eaux thermales curatives. Par bonheur, le Palace Hotel da Curia a su garder son charme et son atmosphère d'antan. Ici, le temps semble s'être arrêté.

Bien que l'hôtel ait été restauré, il a fort heureusement subi peu de changements et offre la même ambiance qui y régnait il y a près de cent ans. Si l'on y trouve aujourd'hui tout le confort moderne, il a su conserver le cachet typique de la Belle Époque. Désormais d'un autre siècle, ce palace majestueux reste néanmoins une création encore bien jeune dans cette région gorgée d'histoire.

Beiras sur la côte atlantique est une des contrées les moins connues du Portugal, encore hors des sentiers battus. Située sur la côte occidentale, elle fait partie des régions les plus diversifiées du pays, alliant montagnes et vallées verdoyantes, villages paisibles et longs rivages de sable.

Livre à emporter : « Histoire du siège de Lisbonne » de José Saramago

ANREISE	20 km nördlich von Coimbra, 2 Stunden nördlich von Lissabon und 1 Stunde südlich von Porto entfernt
PREIS	Zwischen 75 und 90 €, Frühstück inklusive
ZIMMER	114 Zimmer
KÜCHE	Lokale Spezialitäten und klassische internationale Küche
GESCHICHTE	Erbaut in den 1920er Jahren, eröffnet 1926
X-FAKTOR	Flair der Belle Époque

ACCÈS	À 20 km au nord de Coïmbra; à 2 heures au nord de Lisbonne et 1 heure au sud de Porto
PRIX	De 75 à 90 €, petit déjeuner compris
CHAMBRES	114 chambres
RESTAURATION	Spécialités locales et cuisine internationale
HISTOIRE	Construit au début des années 1920, l'hôtel a ouvert en 1926
LES «PLUS»	Ambiance Belle Époque

Pilgrim's rest

Paço de São Cipriano, Minho

Paço de São Cipriano, Minho

Pilgrim's rest

This house would have been a welcome sight to pilgrims on their way to the cathedral and shrine of St. James, in Spain. For centuries, thousands of people have trod this road on a journey to see the tomb of the Apostle. Walking the long route to Santiago de Compostela, from France through Portugal and then on to Spain, was a spiritual goal. The sore feet on such a trek would be a sharp daily reminder of one's human frailties.

Resting at Paço de São Cipriano would have been a divine treat to look forward to. It still is for many. The ancient custom of receiving guests carries on; the modern traveller or the pilgrim, by car or on foot, is still welcomed here. This former manor house is set in the midst of lush greenery. As well as gardens, orchards, and vineyards, it has its own chapel, and is also blessed with wine cellars. The house is one of the many old noble seats that have been restored all through the country. While most are still family homes, paying guests can now share their proud history. The past is very much part of the present. Here, the tower room, with its splendid bed, evokes the spirit of the old Portugal.

Book to pack: "The Pilgrimage: A Contemporary Quest for Ancient Wisdom" by Paulo Coelho

Paço de São Cipriano	
Tabuadelo – 4810-892	
Guimarães	
Minho	
Portugal	
Tel: + 351 253 565 337	
Fax: + 351 253 565 337	
No e-mail	
Website: www.pacosaocipriano.com	

DIRECTIONS	In the north of Portugal, north-east from Porto. 6 km from Guimarães
RATES	€ 100
ROOMS	7 rooms
FOOD	Only breakfast, restaurants near the hotel
HISTORY	The house was built in the 15th century and opened as a hotel in 1983
X-FACTOR	The serene gardens and sense of history

Nachtlager für Pilger

Dieses Haus wäre ein willkommener Anblick für Pilger auf dem Weg zur Kathedrale des heiligen Jakobus in Spanien gewesen. Im Laufe der Jahrhunderte sind tausende von Menschen hier entlang gepilgert, um das Grabmal des Apostels zu sehen. Der weite Weg nach Santiago de Compostela von Frankreich über Portugal bis nach Spanien war ein großes religiöses Ereignis. Und die vom langen Marsch wunden Füße gemahnten die Menschen täglich an ihre Gebrechlichkeit.

Sich im Paço de São Cipriano zur Ruhe zu legen wäre gewiss ein göttliches Vergnügen gewesen, dem man mit großer Freude entgegengeblickt hätte. Viele können das heute noch genießen, denn der alte Brauch, Gäste zu empfangen, wird fortgeführt. Jeder – vom modernen Reisenden bis zum Pilger, egal, ob mit dem Auto oder zu Fuß – ist hier willkommen. Das ehemalige Herrenhaus ist eingebettet in eine üppige, grüne Landschaft. Neben Gärten, Obstgärten und Weinbergen verfügt es über eine eigene Kapelle und ist noch dazu mit Weinkellern bestückt. Es handelt sich um einen der vielen alten Adelssitze, die im ganzen Land restauriert wurden. Obwohl die meisten von ihnen noch im Familienbesitz sind, können auch zahlende Gäste an ihrer stolzen Geschichte teilhaben. Die Vergangenheit ist in der Gegenwart noch sehr präsent. So lässt das Turmzimmer mit seinem prächtigen Bett den Geist des alten Portugals auferstehen.

Buchtipp: »Auf dem Jakobsweg. Tagebuch einer Pilgerreise nach Santiago de Compostela« von Paulo Coelho

Sur la route des pèlerins

Nul doute que la vue de cette maison n'ait réjoui bien des pèlerins en route vers la cathédrale Saint-Jacques en Espagne. Au cours des siècles, des milliers de personnes ont parcouru le chemin menant à la tombe de l'apôtre. La route de Compostelle, de la France à l'Espagne en passant par le Portugal, avait une finalité spirituelle. Les pieds meurtris rappelaient chaque jour la fragilité de l'homme.

Faire enfin halte au Paço de São Cipriano devait être un moment divin ... et l'est toujours aujourd'hui. L'ancienne coutume d'accueillir les voyageurs perdure : touriste ou pèlerin, en voiture ou à pied, chacun est ici le bienvenu. Cet ancien manoir est situé au cœur d'une nature verdoyante. Outre des jardins, vergers et vignobles, il possède sa propre chapelle et des caves à vin. La demeure fait partie des nombreuses résidences patriciennes à avoir été restaurées dans le pays. Si la plupart sont toujours habitées par les familles d'origine, des hôtes payants peuvent partager leur fier passé. L'histoire semble faire partie du présent : ici, la chambre de la tour, avec son lit splendide, évoque le Portugal au temps jadis.

Livre à emporter : « Le Pèlerin de Compostelle » de Paulo Coelho

ANREISE	Im Norden von Portugal, nordöstlich von Porto, 6 km von Guimarães entfernt
PREIS	100 €
ZIMMER	7 Zimmer
KÜCHE	Nur Frühstück, Restaurants in der Nähe des Hotels
GESCHICHTE	Das Gebäude stammt aus dem 15. Jahrhundert und wurde 1983 als Hotel eröffnet
X-FAKTOR	Die herrlichen Gärten und der Sinn für Geschichte

ACCÈS	Au nord du Portugal, au nord-est de Porto. À 6 km de Guimarães
PRIX	100 €
CHAMBRES	7 chambres
RESTAURATION	Petit déjeuner uniquement, restaurants à proximité de l'hôtel
HISTOIRE	Construit au XVe siècle, le Paço de São Cipriano a ouvert ses portes en 1983
LES « PLUS »	Jardins paisibles et cadre historique

Grace and favour...
Reid's Palace, Madeira

Reid's Palace, Madeira

Grace and favour

For generations this grand old hotel has been the byword of grace. Reid's Palace has served as a home away from home to many of the most well-known people of the last century. The guest book is a roll call of celebrities. Anybody who was, or is still, somebody has stayed here at one time. So little seems to have changed that you can picture Winston Churchill taking afternoon tea on the terrace; Elisabeth, the Empress of Austria, gazing out to sea from her veranda; and imagine watching George Bernard Shaw being taught the tango on the lawn. The old-fashioned charm continues to draw the rich and famous, as well as the not yet renowned. Part of the attraction is the setting on the island of Madeira. High up on the cliff tops overlooking the Bay of Funchal and the Atlantic, the hotel's site adds to the privacy of its guests. Staying here is almost like being on the "grand tour"; but the days of luxury travel are not re-created here, in fact it has always been like this.

Reid's Palace evokes eras that were more gracious and less hurried than the one we live in now. Time has been kind to this lovely old landmark.

Book to pack: "Pygmalion and My Fair Lady" by George Bernard Shaw

Reid's Palace
Estrada Monumental 139
9000-098 Funchal
Madeira
Portugal
Tel: + 351 291 71 71 71
Fax: + 351 291 71 71 77
E-mail: reservations@reidspalace.com
Website: www.reidspalace.orient-express.com

DIRECTIONS	22 km/14 m from Madeira International Airport
RATES	Rooms from € 259 to 496, suites from € 616 to 2619, inclusive of breakfast
ROOMS	130 rooms and 34 suites
FOOD	5 restaurants to choose from
HISTORY	The original hotel was built and opened in 1891. In 1967 an extension was built
X-FACTOR	A destination in itself

Ruhm und Ehre

Seit Generationen war dieses große alte Hotel der Inbegriff von Eleganz.

In Reid's Palace fanden viele berühmte Persönlichkeiten des letzten Jahrhunderts eine zweite Heimat. Alle Berühmtheiten haben – so scheint es – schon einmal hier gewohnt. Und so wenig scheinen sich die Zeiten verändert zu haben, dass man sich noch jetzt Winston Churchill beim Nachmittagstee auf der Terrasse vorstellen kann oder die österreichische Kaiserin Elisabeth, berühmt als Sisi, die von ihrer Veranda aus auf das Meer blickt, oder George Bernard Shaw, der auf dem Rasen Tango lernt. Ungebrochen scheint der altmodische Charme des Hotels wie ein Magnet auf die Reichen und Schönen zu wirken, aber ebenso auf die nicht wirklich oder noch nicht Berühmten. Ein weiterer Anziehungspunkt ist die Lage des Hotels. Hoch über den Klippen errichtet, bietet es einen Blick über die Bucht von Funchal auf den Atlantik und schützt durch seine exponierte Lage die Privatsphäre der Gäste.

Wer hier zu Gast ist, wird sich fühlen wie damals die reichen jungen Leute, die durch die Welt reisen, um ihren Horizont zu erweitern. Aber hier muss die Vergangenheit nicht künstlich wiedererweckt werden, hier ist es einfach so, wie es schon immer gewesen ist. An diesem Ort, zu dem die Zeit so freundlich war, darf man noch einmal teilhaben am Charme und der Ruhe früherer Zeiten.

Buchtipps: »Pygmalion and My Fair Lady« von George Bernard Shaw
»Churchill« von Sebastian Haffner

Retraite des célébrités

Symbole d'élégance depuis des générations, le Reid's Palace a accueilli maintes célébrités du siècle passé, comme en témoigne son livre d'or. Tous les grands personnages ont séjourné au moins une fois en ces lieux. Le cadre a si peu changé que l'on imagine sans peine Winston Churchill prendre le thé sur la terrasse, Sissi, impératrice d'Autriche, scruter la mer depuis sa véranda, ou George Bernard Shaw prendre des cours de tango sur la pelouse. Le charme désuet continue d'attirer les grands et les moins grands de ce monde. L'un des atouts de l'hôtel est sa situation sur l'île de Madère. Perché sur les falaises dominant la baie de Funchal et l'Atlantique, il offre la retraite discrète recherchée par la clientèle.

Un séjour dans ce palace évoque les somptueux voyages de la haute société d'autrefois; mais le luxe n'a pas été recréé. Ici, il existe depuis toujours. Le Reid's Palace rappelle une époque plus raffinée et moins agitée que celle d'aujourd'hui. Le temps a su épargner cet endroit plein de charme et de chic.

Livre à emporter : « L'Homme et les armes » de George Bernard Shaw

ANREISE	22 km vom Flughafen Madeira International
PREIS	Zimmer zwischen 259 und 496 €, Suiten zwischen 616 und 2619 €, Frühstück inklusive
ZIMMER	130 Zimmer und 34 Suiten
KÜCHE	5 Restaurants stehen zur Auswahl
GESCHICHTE	Das ursprüngliche Hotel wurde 1891 gebaut und eröffnet; 1967 kam ein Anbau hinzu
X-FAKTOR	Ein Ziel an sich

ACCÈS	À 22 km de l'aéroport Madeira International
PRIX	Chambres de 259 à 496 €, suites de 616 à 2619 €, petit déjeuner compris
CHAMBRES	130 chambres et 34 suites
RESTAURATION	5 restaurants au choix
HISTOIRE	L'hôtel a été construit et a ouvert en 1891. Une annexe a été ajoutée en 1967
LES « PLUS »	Une destination en soi

VIEW OF
REID'S NEW HOTEL
MADEIRA.

Crossroads...
Marco Polo Mansion, Rhodos

Marco Polo Mansion, Rhodos

Crossroads

Greek myth ascribes the origin of Rhodes to the passion that the Sun God felt for the daughter of the God of the Sea. This love resulted in the birth of an island blessed with sun. For centuries it has attracted all sorts of visitors to its shores. On a small street surrounded by mosques, and sequestered behind shutters, the Marco Polo Mansion is a magnet for travellers and Rhodes-scholars alike. The hotel takes the latter part of its name from the Latin *manere*, which means to stay and to dwell. Here the atmosphere is such that guests can easily be inclined to linger for days. Hidden behind the walls of this little medieval hotel is a cool green garden. Apricot and orange trees grow alongside purple bougainvilleas and red poinsettias in a brilliant blaze of colour. Inside the arched doorways it is just as vibrant, with richly hued walls and furnishings. A mix of Mediterranean antiques and locally made pieces fashioned in the island's traditional simple style add detail.

This beautifully restored house in the old town's Turkish quarter is a perfect base from which to explore the classical island of Rhodes.

Books to pack: "The Travels of Marco Polo" by Marco Polo
"The Discovery of Slowness" by Sten Nadolny

Marco Polo Mansion
42, Ag. Fanouriou
Old Town
85100 Rhodes
Greece
Tel: + 30 2410 25562
Fax: + 30 2410 25562
E-mail: marcopolomansion@hotmail.com
Website: www.marcopolomansion.web.com

DIRECTIONS	In the Turkish quarter of the old town of Rhodes
RATES	€ 50 to 140, including breakfast
ROOMS	7 rooms, all unique, one with a traditional Turkish bath
FOOD	A cosmopolitan mix of Greek, Turkish, and Italian in this multi-ethnic town
HISTORY	The house was built in the 15th century and was opened as a hotel in 1999
X-FACTOR	Historic and beautiful hotel in the ancient town

Kreuzwege

Die griechische Mythologie führt die Entstehung von Rhodos auf die Leidenschaft des Sonnengottes Helios für die Tochter des Meeresgottes Poseidon zurück. Frucht dieser Liebe war eine von der Sonne verwöhnte Insel, die seit Jahrhunderten Besucher an ihre Ufer lockt.

In einer kleinen, von Moscheen gesäumten Straße liegt das Marco Polo Mansion, das Urlaubsreisende und Rhodos-Forscher gleichermaßen anzieht. Der letzte Teil des Hotelnamens ist von dem lateinischen Verb »manere« abgeleitet, welches so viel bedeutet wie »bleiben« oder »wohnen«. Und tatsächlich vermag die Atmosphäre dieses Ortes selbst Durchreisende zum tagelangen Verweilen zu verleiten. Versteckt hinter den Mauern dieses kleinen Hotels liegt ein schattiger grüner Garten, in dem Aprikosen- und Orangenbäume zwischen farbenprächtigen violetten Bougainvilleas und roten Weihnachtssternen wachsen. Wenn man dann durch die Torbögen ins Innere des Hauses tritt, wird man von den ebenso satten Farbtönen der Wände und Möbel bezaubert. Mediterrane Antiquitäten und regionales Kunsthandwerk, die im traditionell schnörkellosen Stil der Insel gefertigt sind, ergänzen diese Pracht.

Das mittelalterliche, kunstvoll restaurierte Haus im türkischen Viertel der Altstadt bietet einen perfekten Ausgangspunkt für die Erkundung der Insel Rhodos.

Buchtipps: »Die Reisen des Venezianers Marco Polo« von Marco Polo
»Die Entdeckung der Langsamkeit« von Sten Nadolny

Carrefour de cultures

La mythologie grecque attribue l'origine de Rhodes à la passion du dieu Soleil pour la fille de Poséidon, dieu de la Mer. Cet amour donna naissance à une île bénie du soleil, qui depuis des siècles a attiré toutes sortes de visiteurs, y compris les chevaliers hospitaliers de Saint-Jean-de-Jérusalem. Dans une ruelle entourée de mosquées, derrière ses volets, un hôtel offre une atmosphère conviviale qui séduit le voyageur. Le Marco Polo Mansion tire le dernier mot de son nom du latin « manere », qui signifie « rester » ou « séjourner », et en effet, ses hôtes s'y attardent volontiers. Dans ses murs, ce petit hôtel médiéval cache un jardin frais et verdoyant. Des abricotiers et orangers y poussent à côté de bougainvillées pourpres et de poinsettias rouges, dans un flamboiement de couleurs éblouissantes. Au-delà des portes voûtées, les teintes riches des murs et des tentures rivalisent d'éclat avec le jardin. Des antiquités méditerranéennes et un mobilier fabriqué dans le style traditionnel de l'île s'harmonisent à l'ensemble.

Cette maison magnifiquement restaurée, située dans le quartier turc de la vieille ville, est un point de départ idéal pour l'exploration de l'île de Rhodes.

Livres à emporter : « Le Livre des merveilles. Les routes de l'Asie » par Marco Polo
« La Découverte de la lenteur » de Sten Nadolny

ANREISE	Im türkischen Viertel der Altstadt von Rhodos
PREIS	Zwischen 50 und 140 €, inklusive Frühstück
ZIMMER	7 Zimmer, alle individuell gestaltet, 1 mit traditionellem türkischen Bad
KÜCHE	Eine kosmopolitische Kombination aus griechischen, türkischen und italienischen Elementen im Stil dieser multikulturellen Stadt
GESCHICHTE	Im 15. Jahrhundert erbaut, 1999 als Hotel eröffnet
X-FAKTOR	Bildschönes historisches Hotel in einer geschichtsträchtigen Stadt

ACCÈS	Dans le quartier turc de la vieille ville de Rhodes
PRIX	De 50 à 140 €, petit déjeuner compris
CHAMBRES	7 chambres, toutes différentes, dont 1 avec bain turc traditionnel
RESTAURATION	Cuisine cosmopolite grecque, turque et italienne, dans cette ville aux ethnies diverses
HISTOIRE	Construit au XVe siècle, l'hôtel a ouvert en 1999
LES « PLUS »	Bel hôtel historique dans la vieille ville

marco polo
cafe

espresso ~ cappuccino
nescafe ~ frappe
greek coffee
fresh juices
long drinks
cocktails
beers
wines
salads
desserts
yoghurt with honey

42

Turkish delight...
Ada Hotel, Bodrum

Ada Hotel, Bodrum

Turkish delight

High above a beautiful crescent-shaped bay, overlooking the cobalt-blue waters of the Aegean Coast, is an architectural piece of Turkish delight.

However, the Ada Hotel is not quite what it appears to be – an expertly restored Ottoman palace, full of ancient treasures intermingled with contemporary furniture and fittings. It is in fact quite new, a clever re-creation by specialists in Ottoman design, resulting in a small stylish and luxurious hotel. Inside its massive stone walls are lushly landscaped gardens, swimming pools, and secluded terraces, and atmospheric rooms that have a genuine patina of time. The star-domed marble hammam – the traditional Turkish steam room – is both a visual and physical treat, soothing the eye and senses of the travel-weary. From the roof-top deck, the hotel's classic yacht can be seen anchored near the private beach club at the water's edge of the small village, ready to take guests on day trips and moonlight sails. From here, excursions can be made by boat or car along the coast of the Turkish Riviera, or guests can stay at the hotel, lounge about, and enjoy being treated like a sultan for a few days.

Book to pack: "My Name is Red" by Orhan Pamuk

Ada Hotel
Göl-Türkbükü Belediyesi
Bagarası Mahallesi
PK 350 Bodrum
Turkey
Tel: + 90 (0) 252 377 5915
Fax: + 90 (0) 252 377 5379
Email: info@adahotel.com
Website: www.adahotel.com

DIRECTIONS	A half hour drive from the beautiful city of Bodrum
RATES	Rooms from € 275 to 348; suites from € 320 to 612
ROOMS	8 rooms and 6 suites
FOOD	European and Asian cuisine, some traditional Turkish dishes
HISTORY	Construction of the Ada Hotel started in 1994, and it opened for its guests in 1997
X-FACTOR	The setting, atmosphere, and service

Türkische Pracht

Hoch oben über einer sichelförmigen Bucht gelegen, mit einem atemberaubenden Blick auf das kobaltblaue Meer der Ägäis, befindet sich ein wahres Prachtstück türkischer Architektur. Doch ist das Hotel Ada nicht das, was es auf den ersten Blick zu sein scheint: also ein meisterhaft restaurierter osmanischer Palast, angefüllt mit antiken Schätzen, die sich mit zeitgenössischem Mobiliar vermischen. In Wirklichkeit handelt es sich bei dem kleinen, stilvollen Luxushotel um eine äußerst gelungene, von Experten erst kürzlich erbaute Nachbildung. Innerhalb der massiven Steinmauern befinden sich üppige Gärten, Swimmingpools, abgeschiedene Terrassen und stimmungsvolle Zimmer. Der mit Marmor ausgekleidete Hammam – das traditionelle türkische Dampfbad – ist mit seiner von Sternen übersäten Kuppel ein optischer wie physischer Hochgenuss, bei dem sich das Auge und die Sinne des erschöpften Reisenden entspannen können. Von der Dachterrasse des Hotels aus sieht man die hoteleigene, herrliche Yacht, die in unmittelbarer Nähe des privaten Strandclubs am Ufer des kleinen Dorfes vor Anker liegt und die Hotelgäste zu Tagesausflügen und Mondscheinfahrten einlädt. Von hier aus kann man Ausflüge mit dem Boot oder dem Auto entlang der türkischen Riviera unternehmen, oder aber man bleibt im Hotel und genießt es, für ein paar Tage wie ein echter Sultan zu leben.

Buchtipp: »Rot ist mein Name« von Orhan Pamuk

Splendeur turque

Perché au-dessus d'une superbe baie, dominant les eaux bleu de cobalt de la mer Égée, se dresse un véritable bijou d'architecture turque.

Il ne faut toutefois pas se fier à l'apparence de l'hôtel Ada, celle d'un palais ottoman habilement restauré, où se côtoient trésors anciens et mobilier contemporain. C'est en fait une construction récente, une ingénieuse reconstruction effectuée par des experts en architecture ottomane. Derrière les imposants murs de pierre de ce petit hôtel de luxe se cachent de luxuriants jardins paysagers, des piscines et des terrasses isolées, ainsi que des salles au décor ancien très authentique. Le hammam en marbre se distingue par sa coupole en étoile et ravira les yeux autant que le corps des nouveaux arrivants rompus par le voyage. Du toit en terrasse, on aperçoit le yacht de l'hôtel amarré devant la plage privée, aux abords du petit village, et prêt à embarquer pour des excursions diurnes ou nocturnes.

On peut effectuer des excursions en bateau ou en voiture le long de la « Riviera » turque, ou tout simplement se prélasser dans l'enceinte de l'hôtel en se faisant choyer comme un sultan, le temps de son séjour.

Livre à emporter : « Le Château blanc » d'Orhan Pamuk

ANREISE	Eine halbe Stunde Autofahrt von der wunderschönen Stadt Bodrum entfernt
PREIS	Zimmer zwischen 275 und 348 €, Suiten zwischen 320 und 612 €
ZIMMER	8 Zimmer und 6 Suiten
KÜCHE	Europäische und asiatische Küche, außerdem kleine Auswahl an traditionellen türkischen Gerichten
GESCHICHTE	Der Bau des Ada Hotels wurde 1994 begonnen; es wurde 1997 eröffnet
X-FAKTOR	Umgebung, Atmosphäre und Service

ACCÈS	À une demi-heure de route de la somptueuse ville de Bodrum
PRIX	Chambres de 275 à 348 €, suites de 320 à 612 €
CHAMBRES	8 chambres et 6 suites
RESTAURATION	Cuisine européenne et orientale, avec des spécialités turques
HISTOIRE	Mis en chantier en 1994, l'hôtel a ouvert en 1997
LES « PLUS »	L'environnement, l'ambiance et le service

Caving in comfort...
Les Maisons de Cappadoce, Uçhisar

Les Maisons de Cappadoce, Uçhisar

Caving in comfort

There are few places on earth like Cappadocia in Central Turkey. Its otherworldly landscape of volcanic rock has been sculptured by time and the elements into amazing spires and needles, amongst which apple, apricot, and mulberry trees flourish in fertile valleys. The first Christians carved churches, houses, and whole subterranean cities in the soft volcanic tufa rock to escape invaders. Perched at the highest point above this bizarre landscape is the ancient hamlet of Uçhisar. Here, once dilapidated cave dwellings in the oldest part of the village, have been transformed into Les Maisons de Cappadoce, ten stone houses. Sensitively restored, their added contemporary comforts merging easily with the millennial architecture, these unique homes are available to people seeking a holiday in a truly unusual place.

You can pass your time as a temporary troglodyte tasting the delicious Turkish food in the local restaurants, enjoying the hospitality of the village, and perhaps bargaining at the carpet and kilim shops. And you can follow the ancient paths of Cappadocia, walking, riding, driving, or ballooning over it, to wonder at the extraordinary terrain spread out below.

Book to pack: "Memed My Hawk" by Yashar Kemal

Les Maisons de Cappadoce

Belediye Meydani
POB 28 Uçhisar Nevshehir
Turkey
Phone: + 90 384 219 28 13
Fax: April 1–October 31: + 90 384 219 27 82;
November 1–March 31: + 33 (0) 563 46 20 09
E-mail: info@cappadoce.com
Website: www.cappadoce.com

DIRECTIONS	300 km/180 m south-east from Ankara, 800 km/500 m south-east from Istanbul; Nevshehir is the nearest airport (40 km/25 m), or Kayseri (80 km/50 m)
RATES	From € 113 to 362 per house/studio, per night, minimum 4 nights rental
ROOMS	11 houses, for 2 to 7 people
FOOD	Breakfast hampers available, Turkish cuisine in Uçhisar or self-catering
HISTORY	The guesthouses have been renovated in the 90s, the first opened 1994
X-FACTOR	Bewitching scenery, enchanting accommodation

Erhöhlungsurlaub

Nur wenige Regionen auf der Welt sind mit Kappadokien vergleichbar. Eine bizarre Landschaft aus Vulkangestein ist im Lauf der Jahrtausende durch die Kraft der Naturgewalten entstanden. Zwischen den eindrucksvollen Felstürmen und -nadeln aber blühen Apfel-, Aprikosen- und Maulbeerbäume in fruchtbaren Tälern. Die ersten Christen meißelten Kirchen, Häuser und ganze unterirdische Städte aus dem weichen, vulkanischen Tuffstein und versteckten sich hier vor ihren Verfolgern.

Auf dem höchsten Plateau dieser Mondlandschaft im Herzen der Türkei liegt das alte Dörfchen Uçhisar. Hier wurden einige der verlassenen Höhlenwohnungen, welche sich im ältesten Teil des Ortes befinden, zu den zehn Steinhäusern von Les Maisons de Cappadoce umgebaut. Diese einzigartigen, sehr stilvoll renovierten Häuser, in denen moderner Komfort und die mehr als tausend Jahre alte Architektur eine harmonische Verbindung eingehen, sind Traumziele für alle diejenigen, die einen absolut unkonventionellen Urlaub verbringen wollen.

Als Einsiedler auf Zeit können Sie sich hier an den hervorragenden türkischen Spezialitäten in den örtlichen Restaurants erfreuen, die Gastfreundschaft der Dorfbewohner genießen und vielleicht mit den Teppichhändlern um Kelims feilschen. Die jahrtausendealten Pfade Kappadokiens können Sie zu Fuß, zu Pferde oder mit dem Auto erkunden, oder gar vom Heißluftballon aus, um die außergewöhnliche Landschaft von oben zu bestaunen.

Buchtipp: »Memed, mein Falke« von Yaçar Kemal

Grottes tout confort

Peu d'endroits sur terre égalent la Cappadoce. Des vallées fertiles où poussent des pommiers, des abricotiers et des mûriers s'étendent au pied de paysages surréels de roche volcanique, où la nature a sculpté au fil des siècles des flèches et aiguilles extraordinaires. Dans le tuf, une roche volcanique poreuse et légère, les premiers chrétiens ont creusé des églises, des maisons ainsi que des cités souterraines entières pour se protéger des envahisseurs.

Le hameau ancien d'Uçhisar est perché sur le point le plus élevé de ce paysage fantastique de Turquie centrale. Dans la partie la plus ancienne du village, des habitations troglodytiques autrefois délabrées ont été transformées en dix maisons d'hôtes : Les Maisons de Cappadoce. Restaurées avec goût, le confort moderne s'intégrant sans heurter l'architecture millénaire, ces demeures uniques séduiront ceux qui souhaitent passer des vacances dans un endroit véritablement original.

Troglodyte le temps d'un séjour, vous savourerez la délicieuse cuisine turque dans les restaurants locaux, découvrirez le village et ses habitants accueillants et vous amuserez à marchander dans les boutiques de tapis et de kilims. Vous pourrez aussi parcourir les chemins anciens de Cappadoce, à pied, à cheval ou en voiture, ou bien survoler en ballon des paysages absolument extraordinaires.

Livre à emporter : « Le dernier combat de Mèmed le Mince » de Yachar Kemal

ANREISE	300 km südöstlich von Ankara, 800 km südöstlich von Istanbul. Die nächsten Flughäfen sind Nevshehir (40 km) und Kayseri (80 km)
PREIS	Zwischen 113 und 362 € pro Haus bzw. Apartment pro Nacht (4 Übernachtungen Mindestaufenthalt)
ZIMMER	11 Häuser für 2 bis 7 Personen
KÜCHE	Selbstversorger sind willkommen, Frühstückskörbe auf Wunsch, türkische Spezialitäten gibt es in Uçhisar
GESCHICHTE	Die Häuser wurden in den 1990er Jahren renoviert, das erste 1994 eröffnet
X-FAKTOR	Fantastische Landschaft, bezaubernde Unterkünfte

ACCÈS	À 300 km au sud-est d'Ankara et à 800 km au sud-est d'Istanbul ; 2 aéroports : Nevshehir (à 40 km) ou Kayseri (à 80 km)
PRIX	De 113 à 362 € par maison/studio la nuitée ; 4 nuits minimum
CHAMBRES	11 maisons logeant de 2 à 7 sept personnes
RESTAURATION	Panier de petit déjeuner sur demande ; cuisine turque à Uçhisar ou possibilité de préparer soi-même ses repas
HISTOIRE	Les maison ont été rénovées dans les années 1990, la première a été ouverte en 1994
LES « PLUS »	Cadre fantastique, logement original

> **abitarelastoria.it**
> accommodation in historical dwellings in towns and in the country, in the north and south of Italy; links to each property, with photos and detailed information; plus interesting itineraries.

> **agriturist.it**
> farm stays in the Italian countryside, country homes restored with hospitality in mind, serving regional food, and offering a glimpse into rural life without having to work.

> **bedandbreakfast.com**
> offbeat places to stay all over the world that offer a different experience (but not too different) from hotels, with detailed information, lots of photos, links to individual Websites and on-line reservations.

> **boutiquelodging.com**
> global network of independently owned hotels and resorts, with a full list of properties on the site.

> **castlesontheweb.com**
> for history buffs, royalists and fantasists; accommodating castles all over the world, from King Arthur's Camelot Castle in Cornwall to one in Jamaica, with ratings.

> **concierge.com**
> the online home of Condé Nast Traveller, the American travel magazine; with feature articles and links to "hot lists" of hotels.

> **culturaltravels.com**
> lists holiday themes such as cuisine and religion, for the culturally minded traveller, with detailed articles and links through to tour hosts for each themed holiday.

> **dolcevita.com**
> tips and information for leading the good life in Italy, click on travel for recommendations on top places to stay from spas to monasteries to farm-stays; no direct links but useful information with contact details.

> **dreamclick.com**
> a well-named site to escape to and dream on, aims to show "the coolest trendiest and most luxurious leisure opportunities"; sorted in themes for holidays, from gourmet getaways to dream hotels; great reviews.

> **elegantrenting.com**
> click on rent-a-location on site, features original and unusual locations to rent, from the Ice hotels in Sweden and Canada to safari camps and hotels in Africa; Old World châteaux and castles to New World ranches in the USA; and interesting Travel Highlights section.

> **ellada.net/traditional**
> Greek houses apartments and hotels built in the traditional architectural style, with photos and links to each Website.

> **abitarelastoria.it**
> Unterbringung an historischen Orten, in Städten und auf dem Land, im Norden und im Süden Italiens; Links zu allen angegebenen Orten, mit Fotos und Detailinformationen sowie Vorschlägen für Ausflüge.

> **agriturist.it**
> Urlaub auf dem Bauernhof in der italienischen Campagna; ländliche Anwesen, gastfreundlich restauriert; regionale Küche und ein Einblick in das Leben auf dem Land.

> **bedandbreakfast.com**
> unkonventionelle Übernachtungsmöglichkeiten auf der ganzen Welt, die besondere Erfahrungen bieten; detailreiche Informationen, viele Fotos, Links zu einzelnen Webseiten und Online-Reservierungen.

> **boutiquelodging.com**
> globales Netzwerk von unabhängigen Hotels und Resortanlagen mit einer kompletten Aufstellung sämtlicher Anlagen.

> **castlesontheweb.com**
> Webseite für Geschichtsfanatiker, Royalisten und Romantiker, die Schlösser auf der ganzen Welt anbietet und bewertet – von König Artus' Schloss in Cornwall bis nach Jamaika.

> **concierge.com**
> Online-Adresse des amerikanischen Reisemagazins Condé Nast Traveller mit Artikeln und Links zu den Hotel-Hitlisten.

> **culturaltravels.com:**
> Webseite für den kulturbewussten Urlauber, nach Themen wie Kochen oder Religion eingeteilt; mit detailreichen Artikeln und Links zu Reiseanbietern für jedes Gebiet.

> **dolcevita.com**
> Tipps und Information rund um das italienische Dolce Vita mit Empfehlungen für Wellness-Anlagen, Klöster und Bauernhäuser; keine direkten Links, aber viele nützliche Informationen und Kontaktangaben.

> **dreamclick.com**
> Webseite mit passendem Namen zum Träumen, die die »gemütlichsten, trendigsten und luxuriösesten Orte der Entspannung« aufführt, thematisch unterteilt, etwa in Gourmetreisen und Traumhotels.

> **elegantrenting.com**
> Auf dieser Seite kann man originelle und ungewöhnliche Reiseziele wie Eishotels in Schweden und Kanada, Safaricamps und Hotels in Afrika, französische Châteaux und Schlösser oder amerikanische Rancherferien buchen; ergänzt durch eine Liste mit Reisehighlights.

> **ellada.net/traditional**
> griechische Häuser, Apartments und Hotels im traditionellen Stil; mit Fotos und Links zu allen Webseiten.

> **abitarelastoria.it**
> hébergement dans des demeures historiques en ville ou à la campagne, au nord et au sud de l'Italie. Liens vers chaque établissement, avec photos, informations détaillées et propositions d'itinéraire.

> **agriturist.it**
> séjours à la ferme au cœur de la campagne italienne, dans d'hospitalières maisons restaurées servant des plats régionaux et offrant un aperçu de la vie rurale.

> **bedandbreakfast.com**
> pour se loger hors de l'hôtellerie classique. Une expérience originale à préparer grâce à des informations détaillées, de nombreuses photographies et des liens vers d'autres sites, avec possibilité de réservation en ligne.

> **boutiquelodging.com**
> réseau international d'hôtels privés, avec toute une liste d'établissements.

> **castlesontheweb.com**
> site pour amateurs d'histoire, royalistes et grands enfants. Hébergement en château dans le monde entier, depuis le fort du roi Arthur en Cornouailles jusqu'à un château en Jamaïque. Critiques indiquées.

> **concierge.com**
> le site de Condé Nast Traveller, le magazine de voyages américain. Articles de fond et liens vers des « hot lists » d'hôtels.

> **culturaltravels.com**
> site de vacances à thème, telle la gastronomie ou la religion. Articles développés et liens vers des agences de voyage spécialisées dans les vacances à thème.

> **dolcevita.com**
> bons tuyaux sur la vie à l'italienne, avec recommandations sur des stations thermales, des monastères et les séjours à la ferme. Pas de liens directs, mais des informations utiles recensant divers contacts.

> **dreamclick.com**
> un site destiné aux amateurs de rêve. Spécialisé dans les « opportunités de vacances ultra tendances et luxueuses » ; destination classées par thèmes, allant des escapades gastronomiques aux hôtels de rêve. Excellentes critiques.

> **elegantrenting.com**
> location d'appartements en ligne, proposant des sites hors du commun comme les hôtels de glace en Suède et au Canada, les safaris en Afrique, les châteaux européens ou les ranchs américains. Intéressante rubrique de voyages « coup de cœur ».

> **ellada.net/traditional**
> maisons, appartements et hôtels grecs construits dans le style traditionnel, avec photos et liens vers chaque site.

Taschen Web Picks: click here for even more places to escape to: Of course there are thousands of travel sites to virtual-visit on the Internet, these are some of our favourites - but

> **european-castle.com**
another good castle site; go to member castles then to castle hotels, good descriptions and photos and links to individual Websites.

> **fodors.com**
supplements the Fodor's Gold Guide book series with special features, advice from travel experts, discussion areas, and links. Great detailed list of hotels, no photos, but good descriptions and contact details, and gives picks for each place.

> **frommers.com**
Arthur Frommer's budget travel books on-line, very good information about many destinations, and detailed recommendations for places to stay.

> **gast-im-schloss-hotel.com**
a few of the best German castle hotels to stay at, links to individual Websites for photos and details.

> **gonomad.com**
for unconventional travel ideas, interesting unusual and off-the-beaten-path destinations with a wide range of outdoor cultural and alternative activities. Articles and top picks worldwide for places to stay, from eco-lodges to retreats.

> **google.com**
a great search engine that copes with most attempts to find interesting places to stay – whether you have the name of a place to enter, or a more general search, such as historic hotels in Russia.

> **hotelgenie.com**
efficient site with short list of hotels around the world, with helpful comments, links to Websites and direct booking.

> **lhw.com**
the Website for a collection of luxury hotels, "leading hotels of the world" both large and small, with photos, detailed profiles of each and on-line booking.

> **logis-de-france.fr & logis.it**
a series of small family-run hotels in Italy and France, ideal for holidays and stop-overs, even on a business trip; with descriptions, photos and links to individual Websites.

> **luxurytravel.com**
2,000 of the world's best hotels and resorts, selected from the best international hotel groups, privately owned properties and highly acclaimed label collections.

> **manorhouses.com**
hotels, manor houses, villas and cottages in Portugal.

be warned, you can spend hours roaming the Web finding great places to get away to; it's very addictive. Just add www. to these addresses, and bon voyage!

> **marketingahead.com**
> castles in Spain, palaces in Portugal, and luxury train travel; interesting sample itineraries.

> **nationaltrust.org.uk**
> a collection of holiday cottages in England, Wales and Northern Ireland, interesting and often historic buildings in special locations.

> **paradores.com**
> state-owned chain of hotels in Spain which feature restored castles, palaces, convents and monasteries, along with modern hotels in special locations.

> **pousadas.com**
> Portugal's historic hotels; pousadas are part of a network of more than 40 establishments that include the rich cultural diversification and the best traditions of the regions where they are located.

> **resortsandlodges.com**
> a diverse selection, with photos and descriptions and links.

> **resortsonline.com**
> top resort hotels and information for the luxury traveller, grouped under activities such as skiing and riding, or types such as spas and castles.

> **responsibletravel.com**
> "holidays that give the world a break"; a diversity of pre-screened trips and accommodation provided by leading tour operators, accommodation owners and grass roots community projects.

> **simply-travel.com**
> photos and details of handpicked houses, villas and hotels in Europe.

> **slh.com**
> photos and descriptions of some 280 small luxury hotels, set in superb locations around the world. Each has its own character and appeal, whether a city sanctuary, adventure playground or spa destination.

> **taschen.com**
> check in here for the best books to take on your holiday; and information about more books coming soon on great escapes around the world. Next, places in Africa, then Asia, then America. After that, maybe Space.

> **travelwithattitude.com**
> eclectic short list of interesting hotels and places to visit, with quirky articles about each one and "links with attitude", to individual Websites and places to see.

> **marketingahead.com**
> Schlösser in Spanien, Paläste in Portugal und luxuriöse Bahnreisen; interessante, ausgewählte Reiserouten.

> **nationaltrust.org.uk**
> Cottages in England, Wales und Nordirland, interessante und oft historische Gebäude in außergewöhnlichen Lagen.

> **paradores.com**
> spanische Hotelkette im Staatsbesitz; angeboten werden restaurierte Schlösser, Paläste und Klöster sowie moderne Hotels in außergewöhnlicher Lage.

> **pousadas.com**
> historische Hotels in Portugal; mehr als 40 Unterkünfte, in denen man den großen kulturellen Reichtum und die besten Traditionen der Regionen, in denen sie liegen, erleben kann.

> **resortsandlodges.com**
> eine große Auswahl an Hotels mit Fotos, Beschreibungen und Links.

> **resortsonline.com**
> die besten Resort-Anlagen mit Informationen für Luxusreisende, unterteilt nach Aktivitäten wie Reiten und Skifahren oder Art der Übernachtung wie Wellness- und Schlossanlagen.

> **responsibletravel.com**
> »holidays that give the world a break« ist das Motto der Reisen und Unterkünfte dieser Webseite; sie werden angeboten von führenden Reiseveranstaltern, privaten Anbietern oder alternativen Interessengruppen.

> **simply-travel.com**
> Fotos und Details von ausgesuchten Häusern, Villen und Hotels quer durch Europa.

> **slh.com**
> Fotos und Beschreibungen von rund 280 kleinen Luxushotels an den schönsten Orten der Welt, jedes von ihnen mit besonderem Charme – ob nun als städtischer Zufluchtsort, Abenteuerspielplatz oder Wellness-Anlage.

> **taschen.com**
> die besten Bücher für den Urlaub und natürlich auch Informationen über geplante Buchprojekte zum Thema Hotels der Welt in Afrika, Asien und Amerika und danach womöglich im Weltraum.

> **travelwithattitude.com**
> eine kurze Liste mit einer ungewöhnlichen Mischung aus Hotels und Reisezielen, geistreich beschrieben und mit weiterführenden Links zu Webseiten und Urlaubszielen.

> **marketingahead.com**
> sélection de châteaux en Espagne, de palais au Portugal et de voyages en train de luxe. Bons exemples d'itinéraires.

> **nationaltrust.org.uk**
> choix de cottages en Angleterre, au Pays de Galles et en Irlande du Nord. Établissements intéressants, souvent historiques, bénéficiant de situations privilégiées.

> **paradores.com**
> chaîne d'hôtels espagnols détenue par l'État, comprenant des châteaux restaurés, des palais, des monastères, ainsi que des hôtels modernes particulièrement bien situés.

> **pousadas.com**
> site des hôtels historiques du Portugal. Les pousadas font partie d'un réseau de plus de 40 établissements reflétant la diversité culturelle et traditionnelle des différentes régions qu'ils occupent.

> **resortsandlodges.com**
> sélection variée proposant des photos, des descriptions et des liens.

> **resortsonline.com**
> hôtels de grand standing et informations destinées aux voyageurs aisés, regroupées sous diverses activités ou divers thèmes.

> **responsibletravel.com**
> « des vacances qui respectent le monde ». Ce site propose un choix de voyages écotouristiques fourni par des agences de voyage de renom, des propriétaires d'hôtels et des projets communautaires locaux.

> **simply-travel.com**
> photos et descriptifs de demeures, villas et hôtels européens triés sur le volet.

> **slh.com**
> photos et descriptions de quelque 280 petits hôtels de luxe choisis dans le monde entier. Chacun a son caractère propre, qu'il s'agisse d'une retraite en pleine ville, d'un terrain d'aventure ou d'une station thermale.

> **taschen.com**
> vous trouverez ici les meilleurs livres à emporter en vacances et des informations sur les ouvrages de voyage à paraître. Également, des sites en Afrique, en Asie et en Amérique. Prochaine destination : l'espace ?...

> **travelwithattitude.com**
> liste succincte et éclectique d'hôtels et de sites touristiques d'intérêt, agrémentée d'articles sur chacun d'entre eux ainsi que de liens vers d'autres sites et lieux à visiter.

Taschen Web-Tipps:
Klicken Sie hier, um zu weiteren Traumdestinationen zu gelangen: Natürlich hält das Internet tausende virtueller Reiseziele bereit. Hier finden Sie einige unserer Favoriten. Doch seien Sie gewarnt: Man kann viele Stunden mit der Suche nach den schönsten Urlaubszielen verbringen – es macht süchtig! Setzen Sie den angegebenen Adressen einfach ein www. voran und dann bon voyage.

La sélection internet de Taschen :
Cliquez ici pour découvrir de nombreuses autres destinations : Parmi les milliers de sites de voyage qui existent à l'heure actuelle sur Internet, voici certains de nos préférés. Sachez toutefois que chercher une destination de vacances sur Internet est une activité fort absorbante ! Il suffit d'ajouter www. aux adresses suivantes pour plonger dans le monde du voyage virtuel ...

Photo Credits | Fotonachweis
Crédits photographiques

© 2002 TASCHEN GmbH
Hohenzollernring 53, D-50672 Köln
www.taschen.com

DESIGN:	Lambert und Lambert, Düsseldorf
PROJECT MANAGER:	Stephanie Bischoff, Cologne
LITHOGRAPH MANAGER:	Thomas Grell, Cologne
TEXT EDITED:	Juliane Stollreiter/Delius Producing Berlin;
	First Edition Translations Ltd.,Cambridge
GERMAN TRANSLATION:	Claudia Egdorf, Düsseldorf;
	Gabriele-Sabine Gugetzer, Hamburg
FRENCH TRANSLATION:	Delphine Nègre-Bouvet, Paris
PRINTED IN	Spain
ISBN	3-8228-5889-7

We cannot assume liability for any inaccuracies
which may be contained in the information provided.
Für die Richtigkeit der mitgeteilten Informationen
können wir keine Haftung übernehmen.
Nous ne pouvons être tenus responsables de la
véracité des informations communiquées.